BROKEN, ABUSED AND LEFT FOR DEAD

Breaking Free of Domestic Abuse and Suffering

By

MAXINE ENGLISH

Disclaimer

This book is designed to provide information and motivation to our readers. It is sold with the understanding that the author and publisher are not engaged to render any type of psychological, legal, or any other kind of professional advice. The content is the sole expression and opinion of its author. Neither the publisher nor the individual author(s) shall be liable for any physical, psychological, emotional, financial, or commercial damages, including, but not limited to, special, incidental, consequential or other damages. Our views and rights are the same: You are responsible for your own choices, actions, and results.

The content of the book is solely written by the author.

DVG STAR Publishing are not liable for the content of the book.

Published by DVG STAR PUBLISHING

www.dvgstar.com

email us at info@dvgstar.com

DVG STAR
Dream ► Vision ► Goal
YOUR GOAL IS OUR MISSION

ISBN: 1-912547-30-9
ISBN-13: 978-1-912547-30-2

DEDICATION & ACKNOWLEDMENTS

I would like to dedicate this book to my two fantastic children Ryan and Jasmin who have gone through so many challenges in their lives; some things that no children should ever have to see or experience. I want to give you both a special thank you for loving me even when I haven't always been there, when I worked too hard, and through my mistakes.

Parents don't get given a manual when children are born. But, I've always done the best that I can do, and I've always done it for you both, so we can have a better life.

You two are the best things that have ever happened to me and I love you both dearly with all my heart. I will always be there for you no matter what.
This may be by your side, in your heart, in your head or in spirit.

I want to also dedicate this to my wonderful Mum. We went through many, many years of ups and downs throughout my teenage years, but I didn't turn out so bad. I want to thank you for everything you have done for me. Without your help with the children I wouldn't have accomplished half the stuff I have today, and I would not be writing this to you either as I would never have had the chance to do it. You are my world and I will always be there for you like you have been there for me, unconditionally, without complaint and unselfishly. Thank you.

I want to also dedicate this to my Dad for if it wasn't for you, I wouldn't be the Worrier I am today.
We had our battles but I'm glad I got to spend the last few years with you as we should have been.
We made our peace and I hope you are still as proud of me today as you were when we had our last conversation before you left this earth.

I also want to mention my Brother Ian, who got taken from us too soon, for making my childhood special and making me laugh whenever he could.

For my Nanny English, for being amazing and special to me in every way possible; I miss you.

For my Nanny Laura, who made me feel loved and would let me stay when I didn't want to go home, you kept me safe.

Thank you Gary for always being my friend and helping me and the kids any time we have needed it, my Dad would be proud of you for keeping your promise to him.
Dawn, thank you for being a wonderful friend; we always find ourselves back with each other.

Thank you to Adam Stott for always believing in me even when I didn't do as I'm told, or I procrastinated far too long on things.
You never gave up on me; you knew I could do it.
I appreciate that, so thank you.

Thank you, Sue Davison, for opening my mind, helping me to see my full potential and by showing me how to follow the right path. Without you I would of never have started this journey of self-discovery.

Thank you to James Bayford, for the picture you took of me for my front cover

..

CONTENTS

I AM WRITING THIS BOOK OF MY LIFE. WHY? YOU ASK.......

Because I've had a life of extreme ups and downs coping with fear, low self-esteem and confidence issues amongst others.

I was stuck for many years, and I thought it was about time I told my story to help others that have been through or are going through similar situations that I have been through in my life.

While I tell you my story, I will also be including a section on my thoughts and tips. I have added these to the end of chapters. I really wish that I had this information when I was going through my most challenging issues. I give you my thoughts on what went on, how I look at the situation now, how I overcame it then and what I would have done differently if I could go back and rewrite the experience.

I am an International award-winning transformational public speaker who wants to help a million people with issues of low self-esteem, fear and confidence issues. Once you have read my book you will see and understand why I want to help as many people as I can. I hope you find this book of value.

You will ride the waves of emotion with me, as I give you insight on how I coped with my roller-coaster life, to help YOU get back on track.

CHAPTER 1
THE PAIN HELD WITHIN

I was born in Basildon, Essex on Wednesday 15th November 1978. Dad worked at Tilbury docks on the jetty and Mum had worked previously in Bata shoe factory. When they met they were both going through messy divorces. Mum had a daughter from her first marriage and Dad had 6 children with his previous wife (five sons and a daughter).

My parents fell in love very quickly and moved in together within a few months of meeting and a year later I was born. Knowing time wasn't on their side, they had another child eighteen months later. Mum was in the hospital listening to the strong heartbeat on the monitor. Hours after my mother had been in labour with my brother, Peter was born with the cord wrapped around his neck, and he never took his first breath.

The nurses tried to resuscitate his little body, but it was too late, he was gone. Dad told them to take the baby away as my mother was in no fit state to see him. Dad followed them, gave Peter a cuddle and told the nurses, "I don't want him buried alone in the dark". One of the nurses took the baby to the morgue and put him with an older man who had just passed away, and they were buried together.

Like any mother going through this traumatic experience, she was in pieces. She had gone into hospital due to give birth to a healthy baby boy and came out with nothing. It was such a traumatic time that my dad made the decision to have Peter taken away.

My mum didn't even get to meet her son or touch him, and she didn't even get a choice when it came to bury him. Because dad had put him in with another person mum wasn't allowed her own funeral for Peter. It was like he had to be forgotten. She really did come out of that hospital with nothing.

It was like she had carried this baby for nine months and he had just disappeared. She couldn't grieve, and there has never been any emotional outlet for her as Dad would never speak about him and she had nowhere to visit to lay flowers.

The reason my Dad did this wasn't to be hateful, it was to save her from the pain; the heartache. A few years previously, Dad had a son who at four months died from water on the brain. His head slowly and painfully swelled to four times it's natural size. They knew he was dying and there was nothing Dad could do. However, by not asking her what she wanted he gave her more heartache. She is still stuck in a depressive cycle of losing a child that she has never got to touch, kiss or even see.

<u>MAXINE'S THOUGHTS AND TIPS</u>

Mum never got over the passing of Peter and when the situation gets bought up you can see the sadness in her eyes and she has a heavy heart filled with longing. She wishes she would have held him, took pictures of him and buried him in his own grave so she could go and visit him and talk to him on his birthday and Christmas. She tells me often that she wishes she had said something to my Dad at the time.

In a time like this; the worst point in your life; despite the amount of pain, take the time to spend those last moments with your child, feeling their fingers and toes, rubbing your hand over their hair and taking every part of your child that you created in. Take pictures of your precious time together.

Keepsakes are also a good thing to have, this could be of a hand or footprints to put in a frame. Seeing something of your baby may also help you think that your child is still a part of you, and you are remembering and honouring them.

All these little things will help you with your grieving process in the weeks, months and years to come. Everyone is different, and nothing will get you over the loss of a child, but it will help you with the healing process by accepting what has happened.

Bottling everything inside will keep you 'stuck' and this is where depression and anxiety sets in that you can carry for the rest of your life. Sorrow, longing, guilt, numbness, anger, hopelessness, loneliness and despair are all emotions that are associated with grief that my Mum still carries with her every day.

Never be afraid of talking to a bereavement counsellor as they are there to help you come to terms with what has happened to you. Don't see them as "a stranger" see them as another friend who's there to help you find a new way to move on.

If you are uncomfortable with that, write down everything about that day. What you went through, how you felt at different times during that painful day, things that were said. Moments that were had. This is another way of helping you with your grieving process. If you feel you may need help throughout this experience, go to **www.cruse.org.uk** they are there to help.

I was eighteen months old, and most people don't remember this part of their childhood, but I remember snippets of my life. I remember laying in my big white wooden cot that was by the wall next to the door in my room and the 1970's wallpaper and brown patterned carpet. It feels so surreal that I can remember that far back.

What was your first memory?

My parents had a section of Mr. Cook's farm where my Dad

decided he wanted to breed pigs, chickens and rabbits. Dad's part of the farm was a big area with 8ft black wooden fences around the perimeter and inside he built makeshift pig pens. It was complete with Concrete slab walkways, hay piles, feeding buckets, and a big space to have a weekly bonfire.

On the other side of the lane, Dad also owned a double height barn, which was attached to the stables, that other people rented out.

On the farm, I remember climbing up the creaky wooden barn stairs to the first floor. The upper level was made up of wooden sleeper boards. It only had a fridge and a sofa and a sink with not much else. It was very dark and cold in there, and I always remember that I had trouble on one section where the floor was split into two levels. One half of the floor was higher by about eighteen inches and I remember the loose wood that sat diagonal between the two sections.

My parents always told me this story growing up. I was eighteen months old, and as I was climbing between the split level, I had pulled the loose wood off the split section and fell straight through it, falling twenty below into a wheelbarrow full of animal muck, scaring my parent's half to death. I was lifted out of the wheelbarrow without a scratch on me; and they used to tell me this story repeatedly whilst laughing their heads off. Imagine what I looked like covered in muck and the smell of me, they used to say to me. From that day they knew I was going to be trouble!

I loved the farm and used to go there as much as I could, I dearly loved all the animals. I would sit with them for hours, having them climbing all over me. I would explore the fields where the cows and sheep were, and I would visit all the horses and help the owners wash them down, clean them out and brush them after.

One of my jobs was to go and collect the eggs in all the hiding places the chickens had laid, and I still remember how they would sometimes feel warm still, but it kept me out of trouble for half hour. It was the only way to play hide and seek, when I was the only child at home. Most weekends while Dad was cleaning out the pig pens, you would see me riding on Mummy pig, holding onto her ears as I would take her down to the other end while Dad was cleaning out her pen. I would have all her little piglets following me. I would be sitting on the hay with a dozen little piglets climbing all over me eating food out of my hands and having belly rubs. I adored them as they were so cute.

I still have pig ornaments to this day as I have so many fond memories of the farm.

Not many children can say that from the age of three they used to ride on pigs. Well, until one day I lost my balance and fell into the pig pit where all the pig muck was. I obviously can't get enough of the stuff!

The whole experience is still so vivid, and after thirty-six years I remember it like it was yesterday. The pit was approximately an 8ft x 6ft square. I let go of Mummy pig's ears and slipped off the back of her at the completely wrong time and into this brown stinking sludge. I remember being up to my neck in this cold, putrid, bottomless pit. I was shouting at my parents for help. I was holding on for dear life!

I was only four years old. I couldn't touch the bottom and I was sinking quickly.

The gate was open, so my parents could keep an eye on me they were about 50 feet away in the barn. I remember seeing them through the open gate.

All I remember is them both sitting there drinking their tea and eating their sandwiches and laughing their heads off as they see me slide off the pig and fall into the pig pit.

They rushed over and pulled me out, I was sobbing, stinking and wet. It was such a cold and cloudy day and I was shivering, but they had to clean me down with freezing cold water from the hose. It was the only water available. Afterwards, they took me home for a nice hot bath.

That was the first time I felt fear, I hated feeling that knot in the pit of my stomach. My heart was beating so fast I could hear it beating in my ears. I was sobbing thinking I was going to die, as the ground was like quick sand and I held onto the side so tightly my fingers hurt until they pulled me out; it felt like forever.

Just before my fifth birthday I started Infant school. I enjoyed being at school; making felt pictures, reading the Hungry Caterpillar book, using blow pens and making nests out of the freshly cut grass at break time.

It was fun especially that I already had some friends from playgroup that were in the same class as me. There were times that I was bullied for being overweight and a few of the kids kicked and punched me, but kids will be kids, I thought. But Mum made a big song and dance about it and marched me into the headmistress's office to explain that I had bruises on my pelvic bone and that it wasn't acceptable and asked me to show them.

The embarrassment, "Mum do I have to?"; you could only imagine how red my face was while I was standing there pulling my skirt down to show her.

Back in the day (when kids would be kids), you stayed out all day and either came home for tea or came home when the street lights came on. I was one of these kids too, there were about twenty of us in a small group of eighteen houses. It was a great little road to play in as a child. We would play games such as Kirby, we would skate up and down the street, playing run outs in the alley ways. The mums used to come out and play with us too.

As a child I had problems reading and writing. I preferred numbers and drawing, and I hated reading books because they didn't make sense to me. M. My teachers would make me read pages a couple of times because I just didn't absorb the words that were written on the page.

I would always be asking Mum how to spell things, now I just ask Google and spellcheck! Oh, how times have changed! Dad never knew how to read and write properly as he missed a lot of school as a child for not turning up. But I loved numbers. I always remember asking my parents to write sums down on a piece of paper for me to work out, and I would do pages and pages of them.

However, I always struggled to read numbers on a twenty-four hour clock. The hardest times that I struggled with on a normal clock were the "twenty to" and "twenty past" and this was one of those days. I had been playing outside with my friends in the street all day, mum asked me to be in at twenty past five for dinner. There were no mobile phones back then as I was only five years old. I didn't have a watch either, so it was more like a guessing game and being that it was summer it wasn't going to get dark any time soon. After being out most of the day I walked in my house with my friend from next door. My stomach was rumbling, "It must be close to dinner time" I thought, so we went in to check.

My Dad came charging up to me "where have you been? You're late". I argued the fact that I wasn't late as I pointed at the clock. It was VI VIII. My parents clock had roman numerals, so at the age of five I was learning the twelve and twenty-four-hour clock but the only clock in the house had roman numerals which made it even harder to understand. VI and VIII looked the same to me, but I still argued with my dad that I wasn't late, but on time.

This made him very angry, "How dare you back chat me", he said. He grabbed me by my hair, lifted me off the floor and put my face up near the clock on the wall about 6ft high to show me how wrong I was and that I shouldn't argue about something when I was in the wrong.

All this happened in front of my friend who was also five years old. Afterwards I stood there sobbing holding my head in pain, with clumps of hair in my hands. I didn't understand why my dad would do this to me.

From that day on my friend wouldn't want to come round my house, as she was scared to see my Dad, and she remembers that situation to this day and brings it up on the odd occasion when I see her.

This was the first time my father physically hurt me. However, it wasn't to be the last; this was just the beginning.

MAXINE'S THOUGHTS AND TIPS

I don't know what went on that day; my father may have had a bad day at work or had a rare argument with Mum, but this was completely out of the ordinary. However, it didn't give him the right to pick me up by my hair and put my face to the clock. Sometimes parents get angry and lose our temper with our children.

However, before you push it too far like my dad did that day, think about the consequences of your actions. From that day on, every time I shouted back at him, dropped a pint of milk on the floor by accident because it slipped out of my hands, or came in five minutes late, I would run upstairs and lock myself in the bathroom just in case he hurt me again.

Knowing how old I was and that I had only just started Infant's school and only just started learning about time there should have been some leeway. Especially when the clock was in roman numerals as well. But none of this was considered before he took the action he did. Not only was I scarred for life that day, so was my friend. What gave him the right to do that to someone else's child? Think before you act!

Recognise your anger signs.

If you feel your heart beating faster, you're breathing heavier, you feel your fists and jaw clenching, your voice is about to explode, there are knots in your stomach, you can hear your heartbeat in your head or your face burning.
Then STOP! You are losing control.

If you feel yourself getting into this kind of rage, find something to take your mind off the situation like a project. Walk away, go for a ten-minute walk and come back when you have calmed down. Take deep breaths, slowly until you feel calmer. Count to ten to cool down. Go up to your bedroom, close the door and punch your pillow. Put some music on and dance.

Once you recognise you have these anger issues you can then learn to control them. This could be in the form of exercise like swimming, running, walking or maybe you prefer Yoga and Meditation; any of these activities will bring your stress levels down to a minimum. Alcohol, drugs, minimal sleep and childhood experiences are some of the main causes of people having anger issues. Sometimes they act the way their mother/father did to them as a child and now they are doing the same to their children. The cycle continues. You wouldn't like your child to be like that would you?

If you feel you have a problem with anger and you get rages like this then talk to a friend or family member, by someone else knowing about this problem it makes you accountable for your future actions. If you don't have someone that you can talk to like that then contact your GP and ask them to put you on an Anger Management course (CBT) or have a course of counselling sessions.

Remember you are in control of your anger and you have a choice in how you display it. Because being out of control causes stress, heart problems and high blood pressure. Mentally it consumes you and clouds your thinking. It can hurt your career and you may take your problems to work and disrespect the wrong person. It can also affect the relationships around you, where nobody will want to be in your presence in case they get a backlash of your temper.

CHAPTER 2
THE LOSSES AND GAINS OF
FRIENDS AND FAMILY

My parents had a caravan in St Osyth, Clacton.

We had one of those old wooden caravans with no running water, one bedroom, a pull-down bed from the wall in the living room, a 1950's fridge and freezer, 1970's wallpaper and carpet; with an orange and brown interior and a wooden orange and white exterior that Dad painted every couple of years.

If you wanted the loo or to have a shower it was a walk to the other end of the caravan site. You just hoped it wasn't raining, freezing cold or at night. I remember taking my towel and wash bag and waiting in line for the showers which could be up to an hour wait. Everyone would stand there in silence waiting their turn.

It was a big building all painted light green with eight showers, over twenty sinks and a corrugated plastic ceiling to let the light in. The toilets were round the other side. They looked like cattle shed. A long, thin, grey concrete building with a door at either end acted like a wind tunnel with green toilet doors.

There was no toilet paper back then in the 80's it was more like tracing paper, and they were horrible toilets to use.

Even though it wasn't perfect down there I loved it. It's the one place where all the family would get together and relax and have fun. At home it was only me and my parents. But my two youngest brothers who lived with their mum would come down to the caravan every other weekend and we would play hide and seek, tag, football and cricket. Ian was five years older than me and my other brother seven years older than me.

We took Nanny English down there every weekend and every school holiday too; she would teach me how to play different card games and we would always argue over who was right. "I'm not arguing with you Maxine" is what she used to say to me on a regular basis.

Every weekend I used to wake up and my first words would be "Nan can we go to the beach I want to go crabbing". We used to share the one bedroom, and she hadn't even opened her eyes yet and all I got was "give me a chance to get out of bed". Mum would be cooking a full English breakfast and I would pester her for the bacon rind, so I could take it crabbing with us. Nan, the boys and I, would walk to the beach beaming with excitement.

The beach was at the end of the road about a hundred yards away. We would spend hours up there catching crabs, running in and out of the sea, building sand castles and enjoying every moment there was.

There were so many days like this so much fun and laughter that every time I think about them, they bring a massive smile to my face and tears in my eyes.

When I was eight, Nan didn't come to the caravan as often as she used to; she would say she felt unwell. Dad knew something was wrong, she wasn't drinking, eating or coming to the beach with me as much. She loved spending time with the family this was out of character for her. I was missing my Nan, she was like a second mum who did everything with me.

A couple of weeks had passed, and she hadn't been to the caravan, my brothers hadn't been there either, everything felt weird as I sat with my parents bored.

"Mum, Dad, where's Nan?"
"Sit down we need to talk, Nan is in hospital, she's not very well that's why she hasn't been down."
"Can I go and see her? I miss her."
"No, you can't go and see her you're too young."
"But I want to see her." I protested.

"No! Wait till she comes out and you can see her then."
I argued but I soon backed down.

A couple of days later Dad walked through the door crying. My Mum also started crying, concerned I asked what was happening as I was worried. Nan had passed away of lung cancer.

I was absolutely devastated. The emotions that were running through my head, I would cry myself to sleep every night. I was confused and angry with my parents over the fact that I would never see her again; her smile, her arguing with me, us crabbing, racing snails, and having fun together.
They took my last days away from me.
My parents would not let me see her in the hospital and I wasn't allowed to go to her funeral either.
I was too young to go to the funeral, and it was no place for a child they would say.

MAXINE'S THOUGHTS AND TIPS

Children have feelings too, however, they find it harder than you to understand what is going on, so they need to be told. What my parents did by keeping me away from my Nan at the hospital and stopping me going to her funeral was the worst thing any parent could have done. By taking that choice away I didn't forgive my parents for nearly 20 years. I never got to say my last goodbyes to my Nan. I was never told anything about what was going on, so I didn't get given the chance to understand and accept what was going to happen.

All that was taken away from me.
You see parents try and stop their kids from experiencing pain by protecting them. It's our job, right?

However, in this situation like before (with my baby brother) now my choice was taken away. They took that away from me.

How would you feel if the closest person in your life just didn't turn up any more?

Imagine this, you have been out for a great family day, the sun is shining outside, and the birds are singing, and it's been a great day of fun and laughter. It's time for everyone to go home, you say your goodbyes, you say, "see you next time!"

It could be anyone in your family.

They leave your house and you never get to see them again, you don't get to talk to them again, you find out they are in hospital, but you don't get told why.

They pass away without you visiting them. How do you feel?

It's the funeral day, you want to go but you are told you can't go. How do you feel?

I know how you would feel, because I felt it too. Upset, angry, empty, confused, the question that's rolling around in your head is, **WHY!**

Imagine how confused I was at eight years old. No matter how old someone is they need to understand the situation and they need to grieve. They need to be given a choice. By taking that choice away from them not only will they blame you for doing that. But it will hurt them for a lot longer.

Every parent makes choices for their children it's a normal everyday thing, however, when you have to make choices that will affect your child's life this drastically, put yourself in their shoes and think how you would feel in their situation.

They are humans with imaginations, emotions and a big heart. Take notice of what they need and remember, yes you do have their best interests at heart, but they are also resilient and can take the truth. It will only be harder on them in the long run.

It's like a plaster you are scared to pull off fast because it will hurt a lot more, but it only hurts a short while and you get over it. But if you pull it off slowly you can feel the pain of every hair that's coming off with it bit by bit. It takes ages to get off and in the meantime the child's anxiety has gone through the roof and they are crying that they don't want it taken off.

Remember listen to what they need from you.

The caravan was never the same after my Nan died and neither was my Dad. His smile seemed to fade, and he became quieter and distant.

My two brothers had stopped coming to the caravan and I wasn't seeing them anymore. I refused to sleep in the caravan bedroom where me and Nan would sleep.

I was so unhappy and very confused that I asked my parents why I hadn't seen my brothers at the caravan for a while.

That day my dad told me that they were not my real brothers but my half-brothers. I was devastated. I remember thinking that they were gone forever. Why hadn't I been told this before?

I knew they didn't live with me and we dropped them round to another lady, but I never asked why. It was the norm for me. I didn't know any different.

My Sister on my Mum's side always told she was my sister, but she moved out of the family home when I was two years old and she was seventeen. She had never felt like a sister to me, we never did anything together while I was growing up and she never took me out anywhere. She was someone who was just there when I was growing up that my parents visited.

I have a pretty lady made out of polystyrene that says "love you sister" that she gave me as a very small child, but that's the only thing I have ever got from her apart from a small Christmas and Birthday gift and card that says "sister" on, and I only see her at family parties.

It would have been so nice to have a sister that I could sit and talk to, share stories with and even talk to about boys. I felt I missed out on all that with her. The closest I got to having a sisterly bond was with one of my cousins who was a few years older than me. We would talk about a new boyfriend she would have, she would paint my nails and put makeup on me when we went around to visit her parents (mum's brother) who also had a caravan, so we would meet down there sometimes too.

Around the same time that my dad told me about my brothers, he also told me that I had another two older half-brothers and a half-sister.

Not long after that I met them altogether at my older brother's wedding reception. That evening was such a strange feeling, meeting other parts of my family that I never knew existed. Seeing younger versions of my dad and seeing the two boys after a year or so it felt quite surreal. I was so excited to see them, but I didn't want to make a scene! They had gotten so tall and looked all grown up. I would only see them a couple more times after that......

<u>MAXINE'S THOUGHTS AND TIPS</u>

When growing up with the truth it's easier to accept what's going on. It's not a shock to the system. The situation doesn't become a big deal 'it is what it is'. However, you get some parents like mine who try and protect their child and don't tell them the full truth.

When it is time to find out that truth it leaves a hole in your heart and then there's the thought process of what else am I not being told. With that comes the trust issues and the rebelling.

A prime example would be a couple who have adopted a child. The parents can go one of two ways, either tell the child from the start. This would make the child feel wanted that they got chosen to be with their parents. They may ask questions about their biological parents out of curiosity of knowing where they come from and they may even look for their biological parents to see why they were given up, taken away, or even if they looked like them. After this curiosity is complete they would go back to their life as before and maybe keep in contact, maybe not.

By not telling the child until "they are old enough" as a teenager or in their early twenties; this could work in a negative way, because they would have so many conflicting thoughts. They may question why their parents didn't want them, what is wrong with them, how their lives would have been different, and why their current parents kept it from them.

They may feel like they don't belong anywhere and go off the rails. These are a 'shock response' and it makes the whole thing a big deal when it shouldn't have to be. However, this is an example, and these are my personal opinions and every child could react differently.

After what had happened to my Nan I was feeling a little lost, they say people come along when you most need them. At school I was in my first year of junior school and I didn't get on with my teacher at all. She used to slap my knuckles with the ruler for leaning back on my chair and hanging on to the table behind.

I was banished to the front of the class and told to face the blackboard for swinging on my chair and talking to the next table. This wasn't the first time my teacher did this to me and I had only been there a couple of months.

The day came, and a new girl started in our class. "Would anyone like to help this new girl out and show her around school and make her comfortable?"

I shot my hand up "I will, Miss!"

She rolled her eyes and told the girl to go and sit with me. She was very shy and found it hard to talk to me or anyone else. I would help her with her confidence I told myself.

I took it slowly and by the end of the week I got a conversation out of her. I asked her what her favourite crisps were as every day I got a pack for break time, but she never got any. She told me Salt and vinegar were her favourites. I told Mum to only give me those, so every day she would put salt and vinegar crisps in my bag for break and I would share them with my new friend to make sure she didn't feel left out.

We became inseparable, we hung around together at school, and after school we would play out together. I would go around her house and play and she would come down to the caravan with me. It was amazing to have such a close friend that I could talk to and have fun with.

MAXINE'S THOUGHTS AND TIPS

Sometimes confidence is a big reason why people won't go and make new friends or scared that they will be rejected by another person. I knew that day I needed her as much as she needed me. I knew I could help build her confidence up and bring her out of herself. Starting something whether it be a school, job, a new group is scary when everyone already knows each other and have their own friendship groups. It takes courage to put fear aside and take those first steps, but once you do it's an amazing feeling, you just need to get over that first hurdle and that's the scariest one.

We are friends even now. We no longer share crisp's, but we are always there for each other no matter what. It's nice to have a friend like that, that won't judge you for what you have done, seen or been through. A pure acceptance of respect and friendship, I love her like a sister.

Never be afraid to take that first step with someone because it might be one of the best things your ever did. You have nothing to lose and everything to gain.

It was 1987, the year of the great hurricane, and my school put on a trip to the Globe. We were learning Shakespeare. I missed a lot of school that year as I was sick a lot with tonsillitis. January came along, and I had to go into hospital to have them taken out. It was a scary time for an eight-year-old not to be with their parents for a few days in hospital.

I got to the hospital and gelled with the three other children in my ward straight away. We were only meant to be in hospital for three days maximum.

I was having too much fun there.
Not many people would say that, but I loved it.

I went in to have my tonsils taken out, two days I would be in after they said. I thought I would stay a bit longer. Eight days in fact, the nurse told me I couldn't go home until I had eaten toast, but I refused. Instead I had a great seven days after my surgery. There were four of us in the hospital room playing Yahtzee till the early hours of the morning.

We would sneak in the day room after lights out to watch He-Man till midnight every night before we got caught out four days later. There were lots of toys I didn't have at home and a big rocking horse that I played on every day.

It was like a seven-day sleepover with friends. All in for the same thing and all stayed the same amount of time. It was my final day. I was home on the 31st January, the day after Dad's birthday. Dad had been busy decorating my room by replacing my 1970's wallpaper with Barbie and Ken wallpaper.

I was a Care Bears and My Little Pony fan, so you could imagine the look on my face when I was faced with Barbie wallpaper. It didn't take long to cover my walls with Michael Jackson and New Kids on The Block posters.

Who remembers what posters they had on their walls?

Have you ever had something planned and it all got changed at the last minute?

Not being the child that likes to be out of control of a situation however, that's exactly what happened.

It was my tenth birthday party and during the day I was I was getting frustrated that Mum hadn't made up any pass the parcel or bought any sweets for the games.

So, I took myself down the local corner shop with my own money muttering under my breath how rubbish my birthday was going to be because nothing was done, and I had to do it all myself.
I bought as many sweets as I could with the money I had and wrapped them up for the party games later. While I was wrapping them, I got really upset because Mum didn't seem bothered about the whole thing.

They were moving furniture about from one end of the living room to the other which I thought was quite strange because it was a 30ft by 15ft living room, and I only had ten friends coming over for my birthday party.

That night I had more than 10 friends come over and DJ Gary turned up with a huge sound system and two entertainers and before long they were dressed up as animals and we were all doing the conga around the house. It was the best birthday ever. It was a birthday party that I never forget even to this day.

Sometimes you just need to go with the flow and have fun. I also had loads of sweets left over for me to eat the next day, with a lot of unwrapping to do to get to them though!

A month later it was Christmas and as always, I was spoilt rotten. I always got a main present and lots of little ones. I've never liked oranges so in my stocking Santa would always put a chocolate orange in the bottom instead.

However, this Christmas I had so many presents,
I got Dad to take a picture because I couldn't believe I'd got so much stuff. Mum put on the excited happy smile like she did every year, she was worse than the kids. But this year something wasn't right, she was quieter than usual, and her excitement felt more put on.

I found out a couple of months later Mum had cervical cancer and she had to have a hysterectomy done. Dad and I spent all our time back and forth at the hospital. We would be with her from the time visiting hours started until they finished every day.
I would sit over at the hospital night after night seeing her lay in her hospital bed ill. Not knowing what was really going on.

Cancer was a big bad word that nobody liked, but I didn't really know what it was all about. I just knew mum was really ill. She looked so helpless laying in that bed and I just wanted her back at home, so I could give her a big cuddle.

If I asked too many questions Dad would get upset so it was better not to ask. But every night when Dad came home from the hospital, he would pour himself a beer and a whisky chaser until he was drinking enough to block out the pain.

I knew my Dad loved my Mum with all his heart. I never saw them argue at all and I could see Dad found the situation hard and wasn't handling it very well at all.
At first came the talking to me harshly, having a go at me for no reason, calling me names. Other days he would be shouting and

growling at me for no reason. It wasn't long that before I went to bed, he would take it out on me with his fists, or his belt. Anything could have started it, I could have looked at him the wrong way, spoken to him in the wrong tone or I just didn't do things he had asked me to do quickly enough. I would go to bed and cry myself to sleep every night.

Not once did he ask how I was coping. How I was feeling, he never gave me a cuddle and told me it was going to be ok. What he did do was say sorry with two, one-pound coins the next day.

Let's just say I never went without.

I decided I wanted to stay with my Nanny Laura for a few days. She was so lovely, and she would show me how to cook scrambled eggs on toast and how to make tea. Then at bedtime we would sit and do a word search together. I will always remember her saying, "Maxine go into the scullery and fetch me some biscuits" and we would sit there eating away, drinking our tea and watching TV. For any of you that don't know what a scullery is, its word for describing a kitchen back in the war times.

Mum came home after a couple of weeks and was bed bound at first and she wasn't allowed to do anything for the next eight weeks. Dad would attend to her every need.

So realistically from the age of ten I bought myself up, doing my own cooking and burning everything until I got used to it. I would sit alone and do my homework. Dad didn't like me disturbing Mum and would tell me not to go and see her, but I would sneak in there when I could.

MAXINE'S THOUGHTS AND TIPS

The lesson to be learned here is don't assume that your child knows what is going on. They are just as worried about a situation as you are. You need to sit them down and explain what is going on and what is going to happen next.

Kids sometimes get forgotten amongst everything else that is going on around us.

They will play you up more because they are confused and uneasy about everything. However, the worst thing you can do if you are going through a bad situation is drink. If you are feeling down in yourself, drink will bring you down further. It's a depressant. You need to stay away from it completely. It might take away the pain for the next few hours but the next day the problem is still there.

Find a way to deal with the pain you are going through by being proactive and if you find yourself in a situation that you're not coping with then go and talk to someone. Either an adult that you can confide in and trust like a friend or family member or a professional.

Never lay your hands on a child just because you can't cope with a situation, that's your problem to deal with not theirs.

They are feeling either the same as you or worse. Include them in helping you make that other person they love feel better too, don't leave them out. You need to stick together like a family. This is the time for bonding, to realise how much family means to you, not to tear it apart.

Dad sold off the farm. He sold all the pigs and piglets to the slaughter house, and I was absolutely gutted. I cried for weeks knowing that he had sent them all off to be murdered. I sat and thought of all the happy memories of being down there.

They had all become my pets for the last ten years. He told me after he had done it.

Imagine how that would feel? That is exactly how I felt.

He explained with Mum being so ill he couldn't keep it going as he didn't have the time or the money to put into it. He told me that he had been made redundant at work from a job that he loved.

With more stress coming onto the family my school work started suffering, I didn't want to leave Mum at home. I wanted to be there as much as I could for her.

Finally, Mum was on the mend after a gruelling few weeks and she was trying to get herself back to normality and with lots of help along the way,
she started off slowly but soon got back into a routine.

Dad would still do a lot of the housework and the shopping, so Mum didn't have to walk into town with her trolley as she didn't drive.

She had taken some lessons before she went into hospital and Dad got her a little Mini that he was restoring for her and I would go out and help him work on the car at the weekend.

But once Mum came out of hospital, she had lost all her confidence and didn't go back to driving.

On 2nd January 1990 it was early hours of the morning and I begged my parents to stay up late, so I could help take all the Christmas decorations down in the living room.

There were so many, Dad would cover the whole ceiling, the walls and a big white tree in the corner.

That night in the early hours while we were still taking the decorations down there was a phone call. It was my older brother.

"Dad it's me, you need to come down to where the new shopping Centre is there has been an accident. Ian's dead! They need you to come down to identify the body."

My dad just stood there in disbelief. Steven died at 4 months old with water on the brain, Peter died at birth due to the cord being around his neck, and now his sixteen-year-old youngest son has just died in a horrific car accident.

He was a passenger in the back seat of his friend's car and the driver was racing another driver while he had been drinking.

The car hit the curb, hit the lamp post, turned the car over and my brother Ian got decapitated because he fell out the back window.

He was the only one who died that night.

The driver went to court, but he never got sent to prison. I was in bits, I couldn't believe my brother who was loving, funny and had the most amazing sense of humour; was gone forever. We played board games together and he would cheat by giving me extra money or he would be cheeky and have two goes.

I thought of all the games we played at the caravan, such as hide and seek repeatedly, water fights and football. So many memories from our time together will never to be forgotten.

Mum and I weren't allowed to go to the funeral due to his mother telling my Dad that
"I don't want them at MY son's funeral",
so, he went on his own with no one to console him and Mum and I couldn't say our goodbyes.

They played, "You will never walk alone" as he was a big Liverpool supporter.

Dad stayed in shock and felt completely numb.

He went into depression and didn't speak to me or my Mum for thirteen weeks, not even a hello.

I would catch him crying when he was on his own and when he did finally talk, he told us that Ian's Mum had blamed him for the

24

accident.

She had said that it was all his fault because he left her, and the kids and it destroyed him.

From then on Dad was drinking more and more.
I was seeing more fists every time he got angry, which was every weekend at the caravan.

He would drink so much that he didn't remember what he had done the night before.

Most of my injuries were to my body, arms and legs so by the time Monday came around there no marks to look at except the few times that teeth went through my lips as I was so shocked and scared.

Mum would say that it was my own fault, and I should never say anything to him once he had had a drink. But things always ended up in an argument and a fist fight. I even felt sometimes he would say something knowing that I was going to react, just so he could have that argument at the end of the night.

MAXINE'S THOUGHTS AND TIPS

If you or a family member are ever in this situation don't go it alone. Get the help you need because doing what my Dad did didn't help anybody.

Luckily my Mother is a patient person and gave him all the time he needed to accept what happened. You are never going to get over seeing your own flesh and blood with their head missing. I couldn't imagine how many times a day my Dad would see that image in his mind.

He needed to talk to someone, but he was too proud. He would say that we shouldn't burden people with our dirty laundry, and what's the point in talking to strangers as it's none of their business. So, he stood tall and carried on but nobody until this day knows what went on behind those closed doors of my home and caravan.

I still have the conversations with Mum that she shouldn't have let it happen. She should have stopped it instead of telling me it was my own fault. But personally, I think she was scared. Not of him, because he would never hurt her, but the fact that if she did stick up for me he would have left her as they weren't married yet. I think that was her biggest fear as she loved him so much.

But no matter how much you love someone you don't ever let anyone lay a hand, fist or foot on your child. No matter what has happened that day.

No person on the planet has the right to hit a child like I was hit on a regular basis, and this was all just because he was too proud to talk to someone about his problems. No man or woman is worth that.

Beating an innocent child must STOP!
And STOP NOW!

There were over 69,000 reports of children being abused last year (2018) don't let your child be one of them. If you are going through a similar situation within your family, you don't have to put up with a person like this. You are not the weak person they are. You are the stronger person who isn't going to accept it. The one thing that's holding you back from stopping it from happening to you or your child is FEAR! You may wonder, what if he hits me, what if he leaves me?

If he does either of them, he doesn't deserve your love anyway and let him leave. It's not worth keeping people like that around you. Because if you do it's like telling them that their actions are acceptable around you and the children and they are not. If you are going through this yourself and you don't think you can do anything about it, it's because you have low self-esteem and feel like you don't have a choice to change it.

You need to go and build that up for your own benefit and your child's.

Fear feeds off fear, it holds you back in so many ways and sometimes you don't even know that it has.

Ask yourself some questions.
- Do you like your job?
- Your family life?
- Your work situation?

If you answered YES to all these then that's fantastic you are one of the 30% of the UK population that are satisfied with these aspects.

However, if you answered NO to any of these ask yourself why?

For example:
Do you like your job? NO
Why?

"Because it's the only job I have ever done.
I don't know anything else"?

That's a **CONFIDENCE ISSUE** – don't like your job then gain the knowledge to move onto better things.

Do you like your family life? NO
Why?

"Because if he/she leaves I will be left with debt or become a single parent."

That's a **FEAR ISSUE** – fear is nothing more than an obstacle standing in your way of progress. Face your fear and everything you need and want is on the other side. You will become stronger and wiser.

We fear uncertainty in our life, but we should be receiving it with open arms, because that's what makes life exciting and we learn and gain knowledge for taking that chance. Look how many fears you have overcome already in your life.

Walking as a baby, starting a new school, making a new friend, passing an exam, going to an interview, going out on a first date, getting married, giving birth, looking after a baby, flying in a plane, learning to swim; the list is endless.

Make your list and then say to yourself what's stopping me overcoming this one, and work on it. Find the solution and work towards overcoming it.

Do you like your situation at work? NO
Why?

"Because I wouldn't be able to do the job I asked the manager for."

That's a **SELF-ESTEEM ISSUE**.

Think of Cinderella. She had low self-esteem, no confidence and a lot of fear. Low self-esteem to think she doesn't have a choice but to stay where she is. Fear keeps her in the situation and the lack of confidence stops her asking for the help she needs.
Don't be a Cinderella.

CHAPTER 3
A MOTHER'S LOVE

It was September 1990 and the start of senior school. There were loads of new friends to make and a massive building to get used to and not get lost in. Within the second week of being there two of the biggest school bullies were picking on me. I was getting bullied for being overweight.

"Come on do the truffle shuffle" one would shout.

They would bang my head against walls, and they would smash me against coat pegs which used to break under the force of the blows, leaving lumps all over me. They would kick and punch me and trip me over as I walked down the corridor daily. This happened for months while others looked on, watching and laughing at my expense.

No one would step in because they didn't want to become one of their victims too. I just went to school every day as a new day; hoping it wouldn't happen to me again that day.

Over the next few months it died down, and finally I could settle into the new school and enjoy it.

A year later, Mum had to go back into hospital. When she had her hysterectomy, they left her ovaries in, so she didn't have to take hormone replacement medication.

However, she had been feeling unwell for the last few months, she was getting constant stomach pains and she was putting on a lot of weight on her stomach area and didn't feel like eating much at all. She knew something was wrong. She had been to the Doctor and they told her to go straight to the hospital. At the hospital they admitted her for further tests as they weren't happy with the results.

The Doctor came to see her.

"Mrs. English I'm afraid we are going to have to operate on you. We need to take both of your ovaries out. There are five cysts on your ovaries that could burst at any time, and time is of the essence." One was the size of a melon, one the size of a tennis ball and three the size of golf balls. Even if one of them had burst there was enough poison in there to end her life.

They rushed her to the operating theatre. Another hospital stay, another round of Dad not handling the situation, and here we go again, I thought! Another round of punches and as I was getting older, he was using his belt on me too, so he could teach me a lesson. However, this time I was a little bigger, I was going through puberty and stood up for myself a bit more.

The problem was that all that did was make everything worse. Mum was in hospital, the bullying at school became more frequent and I couldn't cope, I didn't have an outlet.

Dad was going back and forth from the hospital every evening, then coming home drinking and taking it out on me.
Something needed to change and fast.

I would cry myself to sleep at night, worried about my Mum, worried about anyone finding out what my dad did to me and worried about going to school every day or the walk home where they would be waiting for me just outside the school grounds.

The way to get home was walking out to the back field and to go down four flights of stairs to the underpass. There would be eight to ten girls waiting to pick a fight with me and half the school too if they found out there was going to be a fight there. It was out of sight of everyone apart from the people that were there.

There was going to be nobody to save me if things got bad. I was walking on my own, and I needed to find some friends to walk home with, I thought to myself.

I became the class clown, disrupting lessons and I was told to sit outside the classroom for most of the lesson for being naughty. I stopped doing homework completely and I got a detention at least three times a week. I joined every after-school club I could.

Football, Rounders, Basketball, Hockey and Tennis, just so I didn't have to go home, or I'd have to walk past the bullies at the back of the field by the underpass.

For everything that was happening in my life there was no escape. It all affected my school work, my personality, my sense of humour, I kept changing friends, I was becoming a horrible person in myself and I could feel it. I didn't care about anything or anyone anymore. I was scared to turn to anyone just in case they went and told my dad because that would make it worse, if they told my mum she wouldn't get better, if I told a teacher they would call the bullies in and it would be taken out on me even more.

MAXINE'S THOUGHTS AND TIPS

Don't ever feel like you can't talk to someone no matter how old you are.

My self-esteem had been knocked out of me due to everything that had happened in my life. I felt so low and unworthy of anything or anyone. I just took everything that was thrown at me. I didn't care about myself anymore. Being the class clown was my outlet. I developed this rebellious streak to cope with my situation.

They say you learn everything from your parents and for me that included not telling anyone anything and I just bottled everything up inside, this isn't a healthy way to be.

If a child is being rebellious or naughty don't just disregard them and not give them your time.

Because if someone had come up to me and asked me what was happening in my life to make me act the way I did, I would have probably cried my eyes out and told someone my situation. But nobody ever asked me if I was ok. I never felt I mattered to anyone.

No child should be made to feel like that. Make an extra effort to talk to the children that are different because you may be the only person to do that ever in their life and they need you to ask that question.

Are you ok?
Let me help you, Talk to me.
What's happening?

Your question may have such an impact on them, because they will know and feel that someone cares about them and it could change them back into the child they once were.
You could save a life!

Every child deserves to be loved and cared for. If you have children/nieces/nephews etc. Go and give them a cuddle. No reason, no explanation.

Look them in the eyes and ask them how their day was?
Is everything ok?
Is there anything you would like to talk to me about?

Give them another cuddle and tell them if they need to talk at any time that you will be there for them. You see that little face light up. Knowing that you care and that they are feeling loved. That's all any child wants.

So, I turned thirteen and got my first real job, I was so excited that I was going to be earning my own money and finally be independent.

My friend was already working there and so was her sister. They told me that it was going to be a lot of fun. So, there I was at seven am, on a Sunday morning, waiting for the minibus to pick me up and take me to my new job. It took me to a farm, and lots of smells of the past came flooding back to me. I'm home, I thought.

That was until I got into our unit, and it wasn't until I got there that I saw all the hens in cages one metre wide and a metre tall with five to six chickens in a cage. I could have cried to see the thousands of cages all in rows. There were so many that I couldn't see to the end of the unit, and they were stacked four rows high.

My new job was working in a battery egg farm, a little different from seeing them roaming free! It was disgusting what I saw in that place. There were piles of black maggots in the corners, and the conditions were so dirty that you wouldn't put a dog in there. It absolutely stank of ammonia (chicken faeces). No doors were open and there was no ventilation.

There would be chicken wings, heads, legs that had been ripped off the chicken if they had got caught in the belt that bought the eggs down to the front of the barn. Some would even have fresh maggots on them where the belts got turned off and the body part was just sitting there overnight.

There were four people working there all thirteen to fifteen years old. Each of us had a section of the unit which was cut into four. I was section four which was the farthest from the production line. So, I had to go first.

There were walkways between sections. Each row had a belt which bought the eggs down to the front where I was to where the conveyor belt was, each row lasted about thirty minutes. Sometimes there would be a mishap with an egg and it would come out just in its skin and no shell and I would be cleaning underneath the belt and it would fall through, and I ended up with egg all over my head and back.

I would have to pick out all the animal parts and the bad eggs and clean the area. Sometimes the eggs would fall through the conveyor and fall on the floor that I'd just cleaned it was a horrible job.

Once my two hours had finished it was the next person's turn.

So, one day, it was my turn down to go to the picking area. This is where the eggs were either sent through for packing or thrown away in a bucket if they had too much faeces stuck to them, were broken or had no shells, or if any bits of the chicken were missed. This is also where the body parts were disposed of.

Next was the packing area, eggs were put in a tray of twenty-five, and then six trays were put together and put on a big trolley.

They were so heavy I could just about lift them, and the top of the trolley was taller than me, so I had to lift one hundred and fifty eggs above my head just to get them in.

There was one instance it was my third week of being there as I lifted the eggs up to the top level I slipped and crushed the whole top level of eggs. The problem was that the eggs were still coming down on the conveyer belt to be put in trays. I had nowhere to put the crushed eggs, so I found a side to put the trays on. When I looked at the packing area, all the eggs were falling off the conveyer belt and onto the floor. There was a sea of crushed eggs all over the floor. BANG! I slammed the red button to stop the whole operation. I had a very unhappy boss who had a lot of eggs to clear up before proceeding, and I was embarrassed.

Everything was done by hand by four of us so you could imagine how unhappy everyone was with me that day, as they got out late that day with no extra pay.

They thought they had spent enough wages out with us getting one pound twenty-five pence an hour and working six hours a day, it was slave labour if you ask me.

It paid for my weekly magazines though. I got them so I could stick posters over my Barbie wallpaper. I was at this place for around six months. I had enough of not being able to breath and smelling of chicken poo even after I had a couple of baths. It was hot, humid, and the ammonia in the barn was unbearable. One day, I told my friend that it was going to be my last Sunday of working there.

Let's put it this way, it was a day to remember; we were singing and dancing up and down the barn, I was in with the chickens making clucking noises at them.

When I said goodbye to them, we were in fits of giggles, before we went down to the picking areas where me and my friend had a massive egg fight. It was so funny, and the mess was everywhere.

On the minibus back even though we had been had shouted at by the boss we were still laughing at each other, because every time we looked at each other there was egg yolks dripping off our hair, eyebrows, chin and clothes.

Not long after that my best friend that I shared my Salt & Vinegar crisps with, worked at the egg farm and had an egg fight with, who came to the caravan with me and who I spent all my time with, moved away. She had been by my side every day for the last five years and it was like losing my right arm.

With no mobile phones back then, no computers, and no money to use the payphone down the road, we became pen pals for the next two years. Writing two, three, four-page letters every week discussing East 17 and Take That in most of them. As time passed, the letters became less and less, but we never lost contact altogether.

Back at school I was doing so well in my sports at after school club that I got accepted into the District sports for ball throwing and got third place, with a distance of over thirty-one metres.

At the awards ceremony I got given my bronze medal. This spurred me on to do even better in my sports and I started representing the school as captain of the hockey team, defence in the basketball team, and defence in football. I even went up against other schools in shot put, discus and javelin.

In year 10, I was called into the office and given a pin.

"Maxine you have done so well at all sports that we are making you vice-captain of all school sports"

The reason that this was such an honour was the captain and vice-captain pins were only given to prefects and with my history I was never going to be one of those. I felt so happy to be chosen to be vice-captain that I wore that pin every day with pride.

She even said she would have loved to have made me captain but that was a definite no go. I was on top of the world that I was helping my school become the best in the district. It gave me the strength to start working harder in school. Ok, maybe four years too late, but better late than never.

One day, Mum called me into the living room, saying we needed to talk. She started explaining to me that there was a problem

"The cancer has returned".
She said, with a sad look in her eye.
I could feel my heart beating faster, my ears were ringing, the room was spinning, and I sat there and cried. OH NO...... not again!

"Max I'm going to have to go into hospital for a while, I've been to the doctor and I've had tests and a scan done and I have breast cancer."

I asked her how long she had known.

"Well I found a lump a couple of months before Christmas but because I didn't want to ruin Christmas for you and your Dad, I didn't say anything till January, they want me in ASAP". Within a few days she was back in hospital having the lump removed.

That day, Dad told me that if she didn't come through the operation, he would take all the tablets in the house and drink a bottle of whiskey and never wake up.

We argued about how selfish he was being and that he would leave me an orphan.

He should think about what that would do to me. His answer

was "If she's not around then my life isn't worth living, I can't be without her"

I didn't know if I was more hurt and angrier at him for saying that he would leave me behind or that I felt sorry for him. I lashed out and told him he was weak and that he needs to grow a pair and think about other people rather than just himself. I told him to go and sort himself out.

We were at the hospital and the doctor came and saw me and Dad.

"It's not good news I'm afraid, when we opened her up the cancer has spread further than we first believed.

"She had left it so long and with it being an aggressive cancer we have had to give her a full mastectomy of the left breast and we have taken the lymph nodes out from under her arm, as it was about to start spreading around her body. We lost her on the table today and we had to resuscitate her, she is in recovery right now".

We both just sat there and cried. It hit me like a ton of bricks, I nearly lost my mum! My life had turned upside down.

Mum was in hospital for weeks. She wouldn't stop crying, telling my dad she was no longer a woman, and everything had been taken away of what made her a woman. She didn't want him to touch her, she didn't even want him to look at her, she wouldn't even look at it herself. She didn't want to talk to anyone she would just lay there and cry.

They put her on antidepressants to cope. But they didn't work straight away, dad felt hopeless and started drinking excessively and lashing out at me every chance he got. It was too much, I wasn't that little girl anymore, I had gone through too much not to do anything. I was fifteen years old now and I wasn't going to let him bully me.

Every time he tried to hit me I would push him away, he would shout at me and I would shout at him back, he would get his belt out and come full pelt down onto my legs I caught it and wouldn't let it go.

"YOU WILL NOT DO THIS TO ME ANYMORE! You are weak, if you need help then go and see someone! I am not your punching bag, I am going through this too. She might be the one you love BUT SHE'S MY MUM! I love her just as much as you do if not more. Now keep your hands to yourself!", and with that I ran upstairs and locked myself in the bathroom.

I was shaking, I had just stuck up for myself to my Dad, the one person I had feared all my life, he was a crying mess down stairs. My hand was throbbing with the pain, but I knew things had to change. I'd had enough.

I had reached my breaking point, I wasn't going to put up with the bullying from my Dad any more,
I wasn't going to put up with the bullying from the people at school anymore.

I was going to stand my ground and face each one of them. If they thought things were going to carry on the way they were, they were wrong. I wasn't the one to mess with anymore.
It was my turn now.

The next day my Dad come up to me and gave me the biggest cuddle he had ever given me and said sorry.
That was the first time he had cuddled me like that. I could feel the relief in his body and the sadness in his eyes.

Everyone who had bullied me since I started senior school got back what they gave out and some more. I became numb to the pain. I had tunnel vision, and all I could think about was who I was going to pick a fight with next. I picked them off one by one.

The biggest bully in the school – got left with a bloody nose, bruises all over her, clumps of her hair pulled out at the roots and I grabbed on to her so tightly and told her what I thought of her and her nasty ways that I didn't realise that I was digging my nails into her arms through her puffer jacket and I made her arms bleed.

Second biggest bully in the school – grabbed my hair because of what I had done a few days earlier and punched me in the stomach. I dug my nails in her eyes and scratched down to her chin leaving her in a pool of blood and she had to walk around school bleeding from the scratch marks, that she had to explain to everyone including the teachers.

Bully number three – a few days later while walking around school she pulled me to the floor by my hair from behind and started kicking me and sitting on me. I couldn't do much, so I ripped her tights all down her legs and pinched her skin as much as I could before punching her in the face.

The teachers asked her why her tights were all ripped and that was an embarrassing story she had to tell.

Her best friend told me to watch out that she was coming for me, so she got a slap around the face and I told to keep out of it if she knew what was good for her.

She got her younger sister involved with her five friends and things turned bad to worse.

My friend that had moved away came for a visit and we were walking round to the shop not far from my house and six girls surrounded us, including the sister of the girl with the bleeding eyes.

She told me she was going to kill me, that my life wasn't worth living and that I had nothing going for me.

They hit me with sticks, threw stones at me and smashed my head up against the wall. I still have the dent in my head to this day, but still I didn't retaliate.

I knew if I lost my temper I wouldn't stop. I told my friend to keep out of it and to not get involved at all, because if anything happened to her I was afraid of what I might do to them. It wasn't her fight and no matter what they did to me she didn't step in, she had agreed.

They carried on, whipping me with sticks, throwing stones at my head and body, they stung and hurt but I wasn't going to show them the pain I was in. My head was throbbing from them hitting my head against the wall.

We carried on walking and ignoring them.

Then came the name calling and kicking my legs from underneath me, tripping me over every chance they got.

I could feel my temper rising and myself getting angrier by the minute, but I was keeping my cool and trying to control my temper.

We kept on walking, but they just followed us wherever we walked.

The ring leader (the sister) started talking about my Mum, as we lived down the same road and I just flipped.

I could feel the anger in the pit of my stomach rise, I could feel the heat coming into my face and my ears burning, I could feel my fists clenching. I felt like I was a possessed woman.

I just launched for her.

The next thing I knew I was straddled over her with my feet keeping her legs down, my knees pinning her arms and hands to the floor beside her.

I had one hand over her mouth and nose, and I was punching her in the face as hard as I could with my other fist and I just kept punching her.

The other girls were just beside me, but everything they said sounded like they were far away. It was like listening to an echo. They were screaming at me, "you're killing her she's going blue", but I didn't care. I had no other thoughts and feelings about anything. I was fixated on her and ignored their screams. They whipped me with sticks and threw more stones at me, I knew that what they were doing but I couldn't feel the pain they were causing me at all and I couldn't stop.

All five were pulling me to get me off her but I was stuck to her like glue, I didn't move I just carried on punching her. Something snapped, and I looked up at my friend and saw the terrified look on her face. I just stopped and got off her and we walked away.

Every beating I got, every bully I encountered and every bruise I received. It was like a full-on rage, it was like I had tunnel vision and everything else around me was a blur, I just saw red and went for it. Every bit of aggression that had built up inside of me through the months of torment I had received, she got the brunt of it all that day.

That evening I got home and, in the bath, floods of tears swept over me. I could have killed her, I said to myself. The things I did to her I had no thoughts about, it just happened. I had lost complete control of all thoughts and feelings and had no consideration of what I was doing. I scared myself in that moment. What could have happened if I hadn't of looked up at that split second and looked at my friend, or even if she wasn't there at all.

I attended to my pain, my cuts and my bruises. I was aching, sore and very upset. That was the day I said; NO MORE! I am going to kill someone if I ever lose control like that again.

After that incident, the bullying stopped at school, Dad was happier because Mum was home. We were helping her come to terms with losing a breast. She had a long way to go but he was giving her the strength to carry on. Life was looking up at last.

Until…...

A month later I caught glandular fever and I was in bed suffering badly. I had a high fever and my body hurt all over. I hadn't been at school for the last two weeks. A friend came around the house,

"Come on, there's lots to catch up on from school, let's go out"

I had been in bed the last ten days so I didn't feel up to it. I still felt weak and tired, but we went for a slow walk around town and ended up at the train station. I needed to sit down, and we sat on the train station steps where the bridge goes across the tracks to get to the other side. I was feeling rough and needed to go home and go back to bed, it was too much too soon. I had lost all my energy walking down there, and I didn't think I could walk back.

Suddenly, the biggest bully from school and her friend appeared on the platform. They saw me sitting on the steps and walked over. One stood over me,

"Who do you think you are? How dare you touch one of my friends" I didn't even have the energy to look at her.

I explained I was ill, and my mum had not long been out of hospital with breast cancer. She pulled my head back by my hair,

"No, we will do this now" she shouted.

She pushed my back up to the stair railings, and the other bully got a hold of my arms and put them behind my back, with the railings between my body and my arms. I didn't have the strength to stop her I was feeling so ill. I sat there and cried. I knew what was coming next.

My friend was sitting there next to me. She completely froze not being able to do anything she was so scared. The one standing over me was slapping and punching me in the head, kneeing me in the face to try and knock my teeth out. I just sat there and let her do it.

Pain was searing through my face and my head was throbbing. I just waited until it finished.

Afterwards, I just sat there with blood running out my nose and mouth as they left laughing at me that I didn't even try and stop it from happening. I built up the courage to get up and walk home. I hated my life so much. All I could think of is I had nothing to live for, I could of quite easily just lay on the tracks and wait for a train.

However, even then I thought of my friend and how it would affect her and how my Mum would be in pieces.

There was no way after the operation she would come back from that. She had lost one child already and I couldn't do that to her again. I just wanted a happy life where my parents would love me, and we would do things as a family, and have great family holidays, laugh and have a great time at Christmas like all the other families. I wanted to go to school and enjoy my time there with no bullying. There must be a curse on me, I thought. Nothing in my life has ever gone right. Every person I look at wants to hurt me or the people I love die around me. I wasn't meant to be in this life.

I started locking myself in emotionally, pulling away from people who loved me, not going out with my friends so much.

MAXINE'S THOUGHTS AND TIPS

Wow! If it wasn't my own story, I wouldn't know what to say apart from wow. Sometimes in life you just go with the flow and push things under the carpet and just get on with life itself. This is the first time I have written down what's happened to me over those few months and even I didn't realise how much I had gone through.

When life goes on like that for so long it becomes normality, and this is when people get in a rut and they feel they can't get out of it.

The problem is when I was put in the situation that I was in with my parents, I felt like I had no support from anyone. Nobody spoke to me about how I felt about mum's cancer returning. They would only ask dad how she was doing.

I couldn't speak to the person that I looked up to for advice and understanding because all he was thinking about was himself and mum. After such a good start with the sport promotion, I thought life was turning around.

Then Bam! I'm back down on the floor again.

I had reached rock bottom. I even surprised myself that I was still walking on this planet, but I know if I had done anything to myself it would have destroyed my Mum, so it was out of the question.

If at any time you feel suicidal about anything in your life talk to ChildLine or the Sarmatians they are there to help. Not everyone has thoughts like mine and say they can't commit suicide because they know it will break someone's heart.

Others don't have the thoughts of caring what other people think. Whatever your thought process is don't let it be your last one. You were put on this earth for a reason, you just got to find it.

A lot of people know that when you have a parent, family member or a friend going through cancer you feel helpless, empty, drained of your own life. You're just living every day as it comes, being strong for them. You keep your spirits up as much as you can to help that person through it, keeping any pain you have locked inside you...

I never told my mum what dad did to me every time she was in hospital. It wasn't something I wanted to burden her with, knowing that every time she became ill then I would be suffering even more. I didn't want her to blame herself for being ill and in hospital.

However, that little bit of recognition I got for getting that pin got me thinking. I was worth it, it brought my self-esteem back up that little bit more to know someone else see the "good" in me too. However, instead of putting that to good use where I had bottled everything inside of me, I turned it into revenge. Not a healthy trait to have at such a young age, or at any age.

My parents bought me up not to burden other people with problems and I kept it buried inside of me like a raging volcano, that erupted and everything I had built up inside of me came out.

Fighting is never the answer but that is the only thing I was taught to do from my father. If you can't cope with the situation then you hit out on the people that are giving you the problem. This is never the answer, if talking isn't enough then perhaps take up boxing, kick boxing or karate. They will teach you how to control your aggression and give you a few punching bags to practice on as well. I never knew how to control my temper, I do now, and I also know through knowledge and wisdom of being older, fighting does not solve anything.

Let me give you a few tips on self-control;

- Remember: Your thoughts cause your anger and not the other person in front of you.
- Think: Where are you on the stress scale one to ten?
- Ask Yourself: Is your anger going to help you achieve your end goal?
- Practice: Try deep breathing and relaxation exercise.
- Stop: Being defensive and listen to what the other person has to say, we all have two ears and one mouth for a good reason.

What to do Now: Walk away and calm down.

Sometimes when in a rage you can't think like this, it can be one way thinking. So, think of one thing and train yourself to think it every time:

What are the consequences of me carrying on doing this or taking it a step further?

Think positive to calm yourself down:

> I CAN handle this
> I CAN focus on the good
> I DON'T have to do anything
> I DON'T have to finish this off

Revenge gets you nowhere, it doesn't make you feel better, it doesn't make you big and strong. It makes you as bad as them. You need to find a way to channel all that aggression and any other bad feeling into something good and positive.

How you do that?

Through cleansing the body and mind. This could be through meditation, hypnosis, yoga, the gym, listening to upbeat music while exercising, swimming or even a contact sport like I said before. Whatever your needs, maybe there is a way to channel it.

Once you feel good about yourself again and you gain some self-esteem the revenge will slowly become irrelevant. It's all about changing your mindset to a positive mental attitude.

CHAPTER 4
TRUST TAKES YEARS TO BUILD AND SECONDS TO DESTROY

I got myself a nice boyfriend, a great guy. We got on well and we would go out for long drives in his car. He was nineteen and I was fifteen. We would go to Southend-On-Sea with the music pumping out on the stereo, or we would hang out at his house. I got to know his parents and his friends, and everything was great. I got my first flowers for Valentine's day and he was my first sexual partner. After around three months of being together I decided to have a Mum and daughter grown up talk. We sat down, Dad was at work and I explained that my boyfriend and myself were getting on well that we had taken it to the next level and we wanted to be safe. I asked my Mum if she would take me to the doctors, so I could go on the pill.

She hit the roof, shouting at me that I was far too young to be thinking about any of that and he was too old for me. I walked out the house and went around to his house and told him what had happened. He told me not to worry and we will be careful and carry on using condoms. I thought she would be happy that I was being sensible and talking to her about it.

The problem was where Mum had been in and out of hospital the last few years everything to her at home stood still and she still saw me the little girl I was years ago. My brain was years ahead of my fifteen-year-old body because of what I had been through.

Mum was so upset that the next time she saw him she had a word in his ear. The next few days he didn't ring me as much and became busy when I rang him for us to go out. Feeling confused I went around there, I had to get to the bottom of what was going on it was like he was a different guy. He was always a happy, cheery, chatty and up for a laugh kind of person.

I knocked on his door, he let me in and we went up to his room and talked.

"What's up, you have been really off with me since you were last round mine, what did my Mum say to you for you to act this way?"

There was a long uncomfortable pause.

"Your mum said if I stayed with you and she saw my face again she would get me done for rape"

I hit the roof, I apologized to him and told him she wouldn't do that, but the damage had been done.

He was the first good thing that had happened to me in ages and she took that away from me. I went storming home and we had a huge argument as I walked through the door. "How dare you say that to him, I came to you in confidence to be sensible and honest with you. You should be happy that I even come to talk to you and asked for your help, but instead you go and ruin everything, I'm not ten anymore Mum. From now on keep out of my life, everything I do!!!"

I was so mad at her. Luckily, she didn't mention anything to my Dad. That incident destroyed the relationship with my boyfriend and it stopped me trusting my Mum, and I no longer told her anything I was going to do, and I lost respect for her.

She didn't know about my life after that day, I kept her in the dark. I started going out more and staying out till midnight. Going to over eighteen nightclubs till 3am every weekend and hanging out with an older crowd. It was my Dad that said to her that she needs to let me grow up and he would take me to the clubs in Chelmsford and pick me up, so he knew I was safe.

MAXINE'S THOUGHTS AND TIPS

Looking back at it and now I have my own children age eleven and sixteen I can see why she thought I was too young. Talking to me she would of never of gotten through to me because I was happy with him. So, she had to scare him off and that was the only way she knew how. However, she went about it the completely wrong way because now she had lost my trust and respect.

If your child has come to you with a problem or help of some kind think about your reaction and the consequences before you say or do anything. It took me a lot of courage to go and talk to my Mum about such a personal situation. It was the first grown up conversation I'd ever had with her and she might as well spread my heart across the floor and stamped on it.

I'm nearly forty years old now and I'm still careful in what I say. Because when someone has lost their trust in you and they have lost it because of your words or actions it's very hard to get back.
Trust takes years to build and seconds to destroy.

Remember when someone had given you their trust its precious don't break it. Hold on to it tightly because it will never be the same again. On the surface everything may be forgotten but a trust issue will raise its ugly head time and time again.

Back at school I was in year ten, and it was nearly the six-week holiday, with only a week to go. It was my last one before leaving school for college, so I was going to make the most of it.

Dad decided he was going to take a few weeks off work as he was a self-employed window cleaner and could come and go as he pleased.

We would go down the caravan for a few days come back and then go for a week. The great thing about the caravan was that I was down there so often I had a huge group of friends who I met up with every weekend.

Two months previously I had met this new guy and I started seeing him. He was the cousin of the group I was hanging out with. There were eleven of us that used to all hang out together around the arcades, or we would go into Clacton-on-Sea for the day.

We were all between the ages of twelve to twenty-six. It was nice to have a group of friends that would chat and laugh every day, not much hassle, and have cars that we could go out if we wanted to go further afield.

This is where my love of Bon Jovi started. The Keep the Faith album was the only CD played in the car and we would all sing it at the tops of our voices and laughing our heads off. It was a lot of fun.

My parents didn't like my new nineteen-year-old man and told me he was not good enough for me. But me being me I took no notice like most fifteen-year old's and carried on seeing him.

Even as a teenager my Dad would only give me a couple of pounds to go into the arcade with, so I came back every half hour and sat with the older crowd my parents were with at the club. He liked to know where I was. It was his way of keeping me close.

"Dad I'm going out with everyone tonight I will be back later" I said to him.

"Be back at the van by midnight or I will come and find you" he was in fighting talk mode already and it wasn't even 9pm yet.

I went back to the bar to let Dad know I was back, but the front doors were locked; they often had a lock in with the regulars after 11pm.

There was no way of letting him know I was there. There were no mobile phones back in the mid-nineties unless you were a businessman or had a lot of money for the expensive phone call.

I went straight back to the van at midnight with my boyfriend and my friend. They said they didn't want to leave me on my own on the caravan steps at midnight, so they would stay with me until my parents got back to the caravan.

Everything was closed, all the food places, the arcades etc. About half an hour went past and there was still no sign.

"Anyone fancy sitting on the sea wall, there is more space there" I told them that the sea wall was about one hundred yards from the caravan.

We were sitting up there ages chatting, the tide was in so we walked up to the water's edge and threw stones in the sea in the pitch black. We sat and chatted some more and thinking my parents must be coming home soon we started to make our way back.

Out of nowhere I heard my dad's drunken voice and he wasn't happy. He shouted at me "I told you to be at the caravan at midnight not canoodling on the beach in the middle of the night with two bloke's you slut".

I tried to explain what had happened, but Dad was so drunk that night he was in no mood to talk and when he did, he couldn't even get all his words out properly.

As I got up off the Stoney beach, Dad grabbed my hair from behind and dragged me across the beach towards the sea wall. I pulled away from him, clumps of my hair in his hands.

"What do you think you are doing" I shouted at him.
"You're the one that wasn't there" I was back at the van when you told me to be!"

With that he punched me fully in the face. I picked myself up off the stones and ran to him and I punched him in the stomach and winded him.

"RUN" I shouted to the guys and we got into the car. Mum stood in front of us.

"Where are you going?" Mum asked
"Get out of the car and get in the caravan right now"
"NO Mum he is going to kill me, I just punched him"

I had my mum hanging off the passenger side of the car telling me not to go. Dad was shouting at me, telling me how much he hated me, and she should let me go. Then he gave me the guilt trip that I was killing my mum with all the hassle I was causing anyway.

I was sobbing, I didn't want to leave my mum with that monster, what if he took it out on her if I wasn't there I thought. What if this is going to be the last time I see her.

Mum was crying for me not to go, I was crying because I didn't want to leave her, but I was so scared for my life I couldn't stay.

"I'm so sorry mum I have to go, I love you with all my heart but I'm not going to be his punching bag anymore"

With that, the three of us left and went back to my boyfriend's house where he lived with his mum, brother, sister and nephew. His mum let me stay the night and I explained everything to her in the morning.

She said if I wanted to, I could stay with them as long as I needed to. However, I was still only fifteen, so she made me a deal. If I was to stay there, I had to get Social Services involved and everything will have to be sorted out properly.

I agreed and Social Services came around a couple of days later and I had to explain the situation to them, about what happened on the night that I left and all the other previous times that he had used me as a human punching bag.

The social worker told me I needed to go back to my parents' house and go and collect some clothes. I told him I was too scared to go back just in case he hit me again.

Due to the domestic violence he told me the police had to be there for his safety and my own, so I could go and get everything I needed from my bedroom.

I didn't want to set the police onto my Dad I told him.
"They are only there to keep the peace and nothing else, it's for your own safety and your Dad, can't stop you getting everything that's yours".

I was in two minds what to do. I was so upset with the whole situation I just wanted it all to be over.

We got back to my parents' house, the police were already there. I saw my Mum crying and I looked into my Dad's eyes and I could tell my Dad was ashamed of me.

He was dying to say something, but the policeman told him he wasn't allowed to speak to me. I collected everything I needed, I was crying my heart out as I felt I had let them down.

Would they ever forgive me?
Would I ever see them again?
Would they ever wonder if I was ok?
All these things were running through my head. I was only fifteen and feeling like I no longer had parents. I wanted to go up to my Mum and feel her hold me just one more time.

The mothers love that you just don't get from anywhere else. I wanted to look at my Dad and for him to say he was sorry and that he was wrong to do what he did, and I would have stayed. I even thought it might have given him a nudge in the right direction to think

"This has gone too far, the reason why this has happened is because of the actions I took, I think I need help and go to see someone, or I am going to lose my daughter altogether"

But nothing was said by any of us, so I left.

I was sitting in the back of the car looking out the window. I could feel the emptiness in my stomach and the loneliness in my heart, the feeling of having no parents to talk to. That forty-minute journey was hell and felt like hours.

The next few days I sat around the house feeling sorry for myself, it didn't help that my boyfriend was at work all day, so I would sit around with his Mum. She wasn't a very nice person, and anytime I tried to help it would be wrong, so I left her to it and got myself out for a bit.

Being five minutes from my Nanny English's old house I was reminiscing about the good old days of the caravan... Mum, Dad, Nan, my two brothers, my friends, the beach. I was missing home, but I was too proud to call them, so I just hid my feelings and carried on.

Over the next few weeks I had made a few friends in Whitham and I felt free and happy, we would all go out together in the car or down to the local pub.

No rules, it was great not being told to be in by 11pm, no strict rules as to who I was talking to, where I was going and what I was doing. I was loving it.

Until about four weeks later instead of us all going out together, my boyfriend said he was going out on a boy's night out and I was to stay in the house with his Mum. I had been in the house all week with her. I hadn't seen him and he was going out to work early every morning and then going out straight from work.

It wasn't a one off it was nearly every other day. The one time I did get to go out after an argument he bought a "work friend" with him and he needed to take her home.

Only ten minutes away he said I won't be long. Over an hour later he pulled up in the car park. I hit the roof. I had this feeling he was cheating on me but now as far as I was concerned it was true.

The next couple of days we didn't talk much just argued and there was an atmosphere in the house. It was coming to the end of the six-week holiday and my boyfriend's Mum was asking me what I was going to do about school?

I was meant to be going into year eleven when I went back but I stood my ground and said I wasn't going back. After that conversation his Mum was picking up on everything I was doing, and his sister that I got on great with, stopped making conversation with me. The only person who was speaking to me was his brother.

We had always got on great as I knew he secretly liked me, but he didn't like to let his family know that we would talk quite a bit. He told me that my boyfriend was seeing someone else. It confirmed the suspicion I had for the last couple of weeks. But I had to ignore what he said because I had nowhere else to go.

I was gutted and had to act normal around him, if he found out what his brother told me it would cause more arguments, so I kept it bottled up inside. But, every day it got a little tougher and the resentment started setting in.

The first thing I did was ring my Mum.

"Hi Mum, it's me. How are you? I'm sorry it's been so long I didn't think you would want to speak to me anymore".

"Don't be stupid, I miss you" she said.

We started talking daily over the phone, building that bond back up again. I missed her so much. "Mum, is Dad still angry with me?"

I asked on one of our calls.

"No, he isn't angry Max, he's just very upset by what happened. What must the neighbours think?"

I felt so angry that she cared more of what the neighbours thought than what had happened. I left it a couple of days to calm myself down.

It was just over a week into the new school term. Things at my boyfriend's house were going from bad to worse. I called my house,

"Mum I'm coming home" I said.
"On one condition: you will never see him ever again, that's the rule for coming back"

With tears in my eyes I packed all my things and I said my goodbyes and thank you'.

However, after being there for eight weeks I felt I had worn out my welcome with his Mum anyway, so I didn't have a choice but to do what Mum had said. I got home and went and sat in my bedroom for the next couple of days. I was just sitting there on my bed thinking that I was back at square one.

But this time with no boyfriend, and not spoken to my friends in weeks, I made the effort to talk to both my parents.

Dad wasn't really speaking to me for the first few days after I came out of my room. I went back to school and had to face all the questions from my friends and teachers. Where was I the last few days of term?

Why didn't I start the new term with everyone else? And because I hadn't spent the school holidays with my friends they were ignoring me. I felt so alone but I just carried on as much as I could.

Within a couple of weeks of being back, it all started again. I had found my feet as an adult out there on my own with no rules and Dad was treating me like a child.

We were in the kitchen and he shouted at me, I shouted back. He grabbed me by my clothes and pulled himself up to my face. The problem was I was cutting bread at the time and I had a knife in my hand. I put a knife up to his throat and said to him "if you ever touch me again I will slit it now let go of me."

He let go of me, I let go of the knife and just stared, I couldn't believe what I had just done. I ran upstairs crying, I went into my bedroom and closed the door behind me. I sat on my bed and sobbed, I was turning into my Dad.

NO this can't happen, I'm nothing like him, I was saying to myself. I started to hyper ventilate and I couldn't breathe. I was getting myself into a right mess. I sat in the corner of my bedroom on my bed crying and rocking, I felt so out of control. I started pulling at my hair, I was sitting there and having a nervous breakdown.

Hours passed, I had stopped crying and I just sat there and looking into a space which felt like eternity. I wasn't even thinking of anything, my head had no more space inside to think, my body felt numb and I just sat there feeling like nothing.

The next day I walked in the bathroom and looked in the mirror and I was disgusted by what I was looking at. Without me realizing I had pulled all my hair out from my centre parting. I had an inch bald gap all the way across the top of my head.

I stood there and cried even more. I sat on the toilet with a razorblade in my hand. It will take 15 seconds I said to myself. I dug it into my skin, my fingers were shaking but again all I could think about was my Mum and how she would cope. I put the razorblade back, I went back into my bedroom and laid on my bed.

I've got to get myself out of this I told myself, but I just couldn't, I had no more energy. I felt weak, afraid of what my life was, what I was turning into and what I would become. I had to do something, but what now?

MAXINE'S THOUGHTS AND TIPS

No child should have to go through what I went through. Growing up I thought my dad was the strongest man on the planet. But when I look back now, I see how weak he really was; with his drinking, his actions and that he couldn't go to someone to talk his problems out. He acted like he didn't care about anything when really, he cared too much but didn't want to show that side of him. He was brought up that it was a sign of weakness to show your feelings.

You see my grandad used to hit my Nanny English.

When my Dad was eighteen, him and his twin brother went out and got drunk on their birthday. That night they came home to Grandad hitting Nan again. They both got a hold of my Granddad and tipped him out the window and dangled him outside by his feet from the first-floor bedroom window. They warned him they would drop him on his head if he didn't stop hitting their Mum. My nan left my Granddad not long after that.

When a child is beaten or sees someone else be beaten it stays in their childhood memories. Children are like sponges and in some children, they take on the learned traits that they were brought up with and the aggressive behaviour carries on into adulthood.

My Dad never hit my Mum, probably because of what he saw as a child. But he still had to get his frustration out somewhere and I was the only one around to take it.

I left my parents' house to get out of the situation, I thought he would change. But looking back now I don't think he would have known how to change, he had been like it for so long. He was a very proud man who would never ask for help from nobody because it made him look weak.

I think this stemmed from his childhood that when his mum used to get beaten he couldn't do anything about it; he would have to sit there and watch. He was out of control of the situation so as an adult he became too controlling. This was his way of being strong. But by doing what he did he ended up just like his Dad.

Me running away from my situation wasn't the best idea. However, at the time it felt like the only choice I had. I should have gone back a day or two later with the social worker there and explained what I expected my dad to be like and how I needed him to change to make our family a happy one. Then perhaps he would have got some sort of help and the social worker wouldn't have given him a choice. I missed the boat on that one. Hindsight is a wonderful thing.

My Dad was so strict when it came to boys, and as soon as I got freedom I jumped in with both feet. Sometimes as parents we don't want our children to grow up, so we cling onto them as much as we can to give ourselves more time. The problem with that the tighter you hold the more rebellious some children get, and I was one of those kids. If you stop kids from growing into the young ladies and gents that they are you could lose them too. But if you accept the growth and stand by their side and grow together, they will stay with you forever.

The feeling of losing both your parents even though they were still alive and then having your boyfriend cheat on you I thought I was at rock bottom, I didn't think I could sink any lower, but how wrong I was.

You see when your self-esteem is at rock bottom you don't see a way out of your situation. You don't see the choices around you because everything is clouded. Sometimes people think there is only one way out.

Like before, I thought of the consequences before I did anything. Lucky, I had my Mum on my mind or maybe I wouldn't be here today telling you my story. Most people that try suicide don't really want to die, they are just looking to get out of their situation. If we can help others by building their self-esteem and confidence up, we have taken the first step in the right direction.

Imagine building a wall. The first thing you must do is build a solid foundation. Add the cement and add one brick at a time. Now put that into life.

This is your foundation.

- Connect – With friends and family, neighbours, work colleagues, make new friends, get a dog, develop a relationship.
- Be active – Walk the dog, go for a jog, go to the gym, join a fitness class or join a club.
- Keep learning – Fix a car, learn to cook, go to college, pass your driving test or even learn a different language.
- Help others – Smile and say hello to everyone you meet or pass by. It may be the only one they get that day. Help with a community event or help a neighbour take their shopping out of the car.
- Be aware – Of your surroundings, other people's thoughts and feelings as well as your own.

By building your foundation you would have brought up your self-esteem and you will be building your confidence at the same time by learning something new and meeting new people.

Now it's time to build that wall one brick at a time.

- Brick one – meet up with friends on a regular basis perhaps go bowling or out for dinner etc.
- Brick two – meet up with family you haven't seen in a while and go out for a meal.
- Brick three – start jogging round the block every morning/evening for 30 min

And so on…….

Once you have mastered it, then use your foundation to pay it forward to help others that need it.

When you help others, you are also helping yourself but before you can help anyone you need to be in the right frame of mind.

Think of the aeroplane scenario. You are always told in an event of an emergency give yourself oxygen first before you give it to anyone else. Do you know why?

Of course, you do, how can you help that other person if you are unconscious? Love yourself unconditionally because if you can't see the greatness in you, how do you expect anyone else to?

Remember a time in your childhood that you started questioning everything? Mum why do you keep getting bills in a different name to mine I used to ask as a child "oh they haven't changed the name yet." Is what I used to get, however as I got older, I realised my parents weren't married.

I like a long engagement Dad would say, however, I always knew it made Mum feel uneasy that they weren't married.

I was fifteen and my parents called me into their room.

"We have decided to get married." They said, and most children would get excited about this situation but within seconds I had so many things running through my head.

Why now?
Why wait till I was fifteen?
Why such a long engagement?
Was I even my Dad's child?
Did Dad really love my Mum?
What if Dad gets out of hand now, he isn't going anywhere.

I looked at my parents with a poker face, "that's nice," and a hand shake was all I could muster up. Within days on the 9th September 1994 they got married at the registry office with a handful of people attending as witnesses, then back home for fish and chips.

My parents knew how to celebrate. I asked Mum why the family weren't there, she said she felt embarrassed that she had been engaged for so long and as far as everyone knew she was already married. I found myself a new boyfriend and this time he lived in East London. This made it perfect to keep out the way of Dad at the weekends when he was drinking.

Every Friday after school I would pack a bag and get on the train to East London and spend every weekend at his parent's place. We would go out together with his friends and parents, have a good weekend and then go home Sunday evening ready for school on Monday which worked out perfectly for everyone.

However, it wasn't long before it fizzled out. Like these things do sometimes. I got back into a routine with some friends and started going out more.

On my sixteenth birthday I had a sleepover at mine with five other friends; we laughed all night, ate Chinese food and drank weak cider. It was a great night I had so much fun.

MAXINE'S THOUGHTS AND TIPS

Sometimes in life you really don't want to do something, but you must push yourself to grow and learn. Hanging around people my age was a struggle as I was older and wiser in my head because of everything I had gone through in my life. But until you try it you don't know if you're going to still enjoy it.

So, no matter what, meet new friends and get yourself out there, and enjoy it! Never be embarrassed by your situation it's better to be honest with yourself and others.

CHAPTER 5
A CHANGE OF OUTLOOK, A
CHANGE OF LIFE

One of the guys I was hanging out with, his mum was a medium and she was using the Tarot Cards for her paying customers.

When she was alone, we would sit and talk about what she does; it was so interesting. I would tell her that I would feel my nan around me and talk to her when I felt I needed to.

"Would you like to try?" she said.
"Yeah I will give it a go, I'd never even seen a Tarot card before" I told her.

We sat there for hours going through the Ryder Waite Tarot deck one by one. She would hand me the card and tell me to say whatever came into my mind when I saw the picture.

It wasn't only about what I saw on the card but how I felt about it. It also confused me that I was telling her I was seeing things on the cards that weren't even on there.

Being a very creative person pictures were easy for me to see compared to words. She would go through the meanings afterwards and we would discuss every card one by one.

"You're a natural!

Let's try the Scapini cards; they are one of the highest decks and the most difficult to read as they don't have so many pictures" She was blown away that within a couple of weeks I was reading them too.

We went to the next stage and tried psychometry.

This is where you feel and see things through other people's jewellery but that just wasn't for me it didn't feel right, I also tried this with photos and again it wasn't my thing, clairvoyance was the next stage.

You are always using clairvoyance and everything else you use is a tool to help you along the way. However, everything I would see when working on my spiritual side would be in pictures. I could look at a surface and get the pictures, so I would draw them on paper.

I would spend more and more time with her as she was helping me develop everything I needed to know about working on my clairvoyant and tarot reading skills to build up my confidence and move forward.

A couple of months went by and she was telling me she had feelings for two men that she had met.
One came around to fix her washing machine and as soon as we met there was an instant connection. We both felt it, as we were talking I soon realised that he was in his forties and I was only sixteen, but the connection was too strong to keep away.

He was telling me they worked together in his tarot reading and crystal shop and they were only good friends. My friend explained to him what I was doing with the tarot cards and the drawings. I showed him what I had done previously.

"Some of the drawing you have been doing are of Runes" he said.

I had no idea what he was talking about and didn't know what a Rune was.

Over the next few days this older guy, my friend and myself would go to his Spiritualist shop. We would sit there for hours and have many discussions over my drawings and symbols.

Customers would come in to the shop I would sit next to them drawing symbols and pictures for them as they were giving the customer their readings.

I would get him to interpret my drawings to the customers as well. It used to astound me how my pictures would fit into their reading and their life.

If at any time they didn't understand my drawing right, then they would come back a week later to tell me what I had drawn had been correct.

For example – a broken glass at the stem, a walking frame, a letter, the hospital sign with the staff and the snakes, a rose, a bee.

Some of the symbols were easy to understand for her at the time of the reading and others she came back and told us what had happened. Her husband broke his leg and had to go to the hospital while on holiday and he used a frame and not crutches.

The glass broke in the dishwasher by the stem two days after the reading, the bee was an annoying friend that she had round her that she didn't know what to do about, and so on.

Two months later my friend walked away from the shop after a disagreement between the two of them. I still wanted to see him as he was also helping me on my journey of self-discovery.

I couldn't drive as I was only sixteen, so I would walk round to his house.

We would meet up often after I finished school and at weekends, so that's where the relationship began between us. My friend was outraged at the idea, as they were not talking, and told me she was cursing me that my relationships would never go over five years.

As time moved on we were getting on great my parents were not happy that we were seeing each other and things with my Dad were getting worse.

Dad and I got into a big fight, we were arguing and shouting at each other and fists were flying. I ran to my boyfriend's house to be safe and told him everything that had happened. He went straight round to my parents to let them know where I was and to have a harsh talk with my Dad.

I was still at his house a few days later, I just didn't want to go back. I was getting older and I was getting less patient with my Dad pushing me around so the arguments between us were becoming constant. I sat down with my boyfriend and we discussed me moving in.

Moving in made life so much easier.

School was just around the corner but, I still wasn't speaking to my Dad, I only had a couple of months left until I finished school and then I was going to college.

By not being around my Dad I could concentrate on my GCSE's and try and get a good grade amongst all the problems I'd gone through in the previous years. Time flew, and I was happy; life was good and I could smile again.

Exam results were in, I went and collected my GCSE's – Math E, English D, E, Double Science E, E, French G, Art C, History U & CDT D. Not a great result, however, I was determined to go to college no matter what.

I had the drive and enthusiasm to move forward and nothing was going to stop me not even my grades on the paper.

They didn't explain everything I had been going through the last few years, they didn't explain that I couldn't get my homework done because I was sitting next to my Mum's hospital bed for hours. All they were to me was a bit of paper.

With dyslexia I found it hard to put pen to paper, life was easier in pictures, life was easier doing rather than just being told what I had to do.

Life was easier telling my story to people face to face. But my grades didn't show this.

September 1995, it was my first day at Thurrock Technical College studying Intermediate Art & Design.

I got a GCSE in Art I might as well use it and I enjoyed using my creative ability, so it was the perfect course. Not that I had many options with one GCSE in Art because the way the college worked. Such a big place with people of all ages.

Not calling a tutor Miss or Sir was also strange at first, just by calling a tutor by a first name made me feel so different. It made me feel like I was respected, an equal and grown up.

College was so great and nothing like school in so many ways, it was bigger and better, no petty arguments and no bullying everyone either just walked past each other or made friends with each other it was fantastic.

I made a few nice friends along the way and passed my course with a 'PASS' grade. I enjoyed college so much that I decided to go back again next year to complete a two-year Diploma in Photography and Computer Design; a brand-new course that had just started.

That first year of college I began speaking to my parents again and we were getting on better than ever. Moving out was the best thing I had ever done for the whole family. Dad and I were so alike in our ways that all we did was clash every day. It was so nice to be able to go around to my parent's house and have no arguments and there was no tension from either side.

Mum didn't feel like she was in the middle of both of us either. Mum did explain to me that she did have concerns about me being with my boyfriend, she wasn't too happy about me living with him because he was so much older than me.

She felt embarrassed about what other people would think of the situation, or what they would say. But I didn't care things were

100% better. We all got on so well that for my seventeenth birthday present my parents bought me my first car. Bright blue MK 2 Escort.

My little girl racer car, she struggled to get up big hills, but she was clean, sturdy, got me from A to B and she was mine. My Dad and Brother-in-law taught me how to drive, and we had many hours of me driving around Essex and at the Car-a-drome.

Dad would jokingly take the mick out of me for something I did one time while I was learning. There was an instance where I came off the main road onto a slip road to go up to a roundabout and there was quite a lot of traffic. I was using my clutch and I kept stalling the car, I would find the bite, but it just wouldn't move forward. I was shouting at the car, shaking my steering wheel, telling Dad how stupid the car was and all he did was laugh at me.

I could feel the anger and frustration building up inside of me; I wanted to burst. I had the hump, I took my seatbelt off, I got out the car on the edge of the roundabout and refused to drive saying the clutch had gone.

Dad got in the driver's seat, I got in the passenger seat, we put our belts on and he drove off. I was shouting in frustration in the passenger side, but Dad just carried on laughing, infuriating me even more.

For years Dad would laugh at me and make jokey comments about that incident. It wasn't funny at the time, I was so frustrated, I was angry with him for laughing at me and that I couldn't get the car to do what I wanted it to do. But now I've been driving for over twenty years I can see the funny side, it just took a while.

MAXINE'S THOUGHTS AND TIPS

I knew way back then I was searching for something, I didn't quite know what, but I knew I wanted to help others. By using Tarot Cards I had found something I was good at and I could help people at the same time.

After losing my Nan and Brother I could always feel them around me, I would sense them and feel their emotion. My problem as a child was that I had so many years I didn't feel like I belonged anywhere. I didn't want to just grab onto the first thing that came along, it had to be right. Learning about Tarot Cards was just one of those steps.

As a parent with a sixteen-year-old I can look back on how my Mum felt about the relationship I was in with someone who was twenty-eight years older than me. I know why, it's because I was so young, and I understand that. However, everything happens for a reason, not only did we get on great, there was no immaturity, no arguments, we would talk for hours but also once I was with him Dad never laid a hand on me again. There became a mutual respect between us and it was finally nice to see the side of my Dad that everyone else got to see.

As a parent you want the best for your children that goes without saying but take yourself back to the years of you being sixteen, seventeen. Were you one of the very few who did as they were told, or were you the kind of person who did what you wanted to do because it made you happy?

I knew my Mum didn't want me seeing an older man, but look at it on my side, my Dad stopped using his fists and belt on me and we started to get on and have a proper father and daughter relationship. Was I going to give that up? No of course I wasn't. I would have been mad to.

Always look at both sides of a story before you make your mind up in how you're going to act and what you are going to say because this will make a big difference to the outcome and what you do next.

School was never my strong point and it didn't help with everything that was going on in my life over those years either. I knew everything would be alright no matter what my grades were. For everything we were going through as a family both my parents always told me "No matter what you want to be when you grow up as long as you put your mind to it you will succeed in whatever you do." I've never forgotten those words. I tell my kids the same thing because I don't want them to feel stuck.

Their grades are what they know right now, not what they are going to become. Life and experience play a big role in knowledge.

My son had just gotten his GCSE's and he has also come out with 1 GCSE in Math. I didn't scream and shout at him that he should have done better. I told him to go for what he wants. He is now studying Level 1 in Catering at College and loving it. He is also dyslexic and finds it hard to put things onto paper but it's all in his head waiting to come out. He expresses it with his food that he makes and everything he has made so far has been amazing.

Life is not all about grades on a paper to show how great you are. You must believe you are great, and you will achieve whatever you want.

I didn't get the best grades in the world but knowing I could be whatever I wanted to be was everything I needed to succeed, going to college was the making of me. I found a place to make friends and not be bullied, to have fun and learn. It showed me how people really are, I grew as a person, I became confident, my self-esteem hit new heights and I even went and saw the college councilor about everything I had been through just because she was on campus and available. After the session she told me with everything I have been through in my life I could help other people gain the confidence I had and be proud of who they are becoming. It gave me a little bit more recognition to use now and as I get older.

I look on with fond memories of that time with my Dad teaching me how to drive. I had no hate towards him, he was my Dad. I didn't want revenge on past mistakes I just enjoyed the moment.

The days we were together doing something positive and I felt loved and cherished for the first time in a very long time.

Hate and resentment grow inside a person and makes you very ugly to the outside world. Don't be that person, forgive and move on. I'm not asking you to forget what happens because that is where we learn and grow, but forgiving helps you to move in the right direction on your journey of life.

So, back to college for my photography course; it was the first time it had ran at the college, so we were the guinea pigs. The only problem was the tutor we had was seriously ill and he was back and forth to the hospital every week.

So, most of the time we were left to our own devices. Put it this way, over the next two years I found a great group of friends in the common room where we would all hang around.

I became great at pool, computer games and pin ball, but I didn't do so well with my 'Pass' grade at the end of the year. I had to catch up and quickly or I would fail next year.

Year two I struggled with college because I didn't know the basics of photography and this year we were developing colour and black and white negatives and photos. Working with models, light boxes and different studio work I had to knuckle down. However, the tutor left permanently, and the computer tutor took over but, he was only with us two days a week.

Again, I was falling behind, I lost all confidence in myself on the course and went back into the common room. I felt like giving up. I had even told my parents that I was leaving but like parents do they talked some sense into me, "You only have a few months left of the course, you might as well stay and at least get a pass otherwise you have just wasted the last year and a half" So after much deliberation that's what I did.

I just wanted to do more than just go to college. After college, I wanted to go into Forensic Photography, but after a visit to the local police station I found out I only had a 5%-10% chance of doing that job and I had to be in the force for five years.

I was bored and I needed something that I enjoyed, I wanted to earn money and do different things, even work part time to take my mind off just college.

I got a job at Electronics Boutique selling PS1 and games over the Christmas period. I got the bug, I wanted to work while I was at college.

I spoke to my boyfriend about it, within the next month we opened a small crystal shop not far from my college in Essex, he would be there during the day and I would work there after college, at the weekends and half term.

To build the money up, we also had a clairvoyance evening every Tuesday, Circle on Wednesday with twenty members, quarterly psychic fayres and we would go and do other outside events too.

I enjoyed being my own boss and making the decisions in what came next in the business.
Until this happened, and it all fell to pieces.

We had an all-day event on a Sunday, it was so late when we got in that we decided to leave the stock in the boot of my car overnight and get it out first thing in the morning. It wasn't on show, so we didn't worry.

I got up the next morning and on the way to college I saw my boyfriend at his friend's house,

"Did you take the stock out the car this morning? I don't want it to get stolen."

He said, "oops I forgot, knowing my luck it will be the car that gets stolen and the stock" I shouldn't have tempted fate, but I did. I pulled up into the college car park and went to lesson.

I needed to go back to my car at lunchtime as I had forgotten some coursework and to my horror my car was gone! I was panicking, I couldn't afford a new car, my insurance would be sky high, I was only third party, so no money was coming back from the insurance company, my stock was all gone, and I couldn't get back and forth to college.

All this was running through my head while I searched the whole car park, to find nothing. I was gutted, I rang my boyfriend, crying down the phone asking to be picked up. That will be the last thing I ever say in jest.

We never found the car again, my Dad was upset because that was a present, I was upset because I had lost my independence and my boyfriend was upset because he had to take me and pick me up from college every day.

The one big problem I did have because all my stock was in the car as well, I couldn't afford to replace it and the stock wasn't covered on the insurance because it wasn't in transport to or from an event, so I had to give up the crystal shop. I learned a hard lesson that day.

My eighteenth birthday was coming up and I had invited a few friends out for the evening to go clubbing in Chelmsford, Essex. After a lot of back and forth, only one friend and her boyfriend could make it, so the three of us went out that night and danced the night away.

There was a college trip coming up and my parents gave me the option to either go to Barcelona for five days with the Art

Department or go on our first family holiday abroad to Benidorm with the crowd at the caravan. I spoke to some friends as I was in two minds as to what to do.

Dad was going to be drinking and I didn't want to spoil what we had built up. One of my friends who came to my eighteenth birthday, was also going to Barcelona and she was so happy I was going,

"I can't believe you're going to be there too! Yay! We can do loads of stuff in the day and we can go out together in the evening and look around".

My mind was made up. Now it was just telling my parents that I wasn't going with them, but with the college to Barcelona. We all got on the coach and it took twenty-four hours to get there with a stopover at Dijon in France for the night in a cheap hotel, so we could all get some sleep.

When we got to Barcelona I fell in love with the place and out of love with my friend. As soon as we got off the coach, we had to partner up with the people we were staying with in a room. She went and stood with another girl and said to me,

"Oh, this is one of the girls from my class, she doesn't have anyone to share a room with, you can stay with her."

I was furious.

"I have turned down a holiday with my family to be on this college trip and the only person I know is you and your buddying up with someone else! Are you for real?" I shouted at her.

To keep the peace, she shared a room with me. Well not quite, none of her stuff got to the room and I didn't see her for the whole five days unless the classes were doing a tour together, I was alone the whole trip.

That week I fell in love with architecture, Barcelona was amazing. Our hotel was just off the La Rambla.

It was so busy in the day and in the night, with street artist's doing the most amazing drawings straight onto the pavement, musicians playing their music, caricature artists drawing people's portraits, and street dancers and entertainers.

The streets were spotless, and the palm trees lined up and down the street. The market places were just as good, everything so fresh and the fish had been caught that day and all the fruit and veg were lined up perfectly straight and in colour order.

I visited places like Sagrada Familia, La Rambla, Casa Mila and the Salvador Dali museum. So many beautiful places to look at I just wished I hadn't of walked around them all on my own.

Evenings were the worst as everyone was going out together and I was just sitting in my hotel room alone.

Being in a different country for the first time and being alone at the age of eighteen wasn't very nice.

By day three I rang my parents and told them the situation and I sat on the phone just crying.

"I want to come home" I told them.

With only a couple of days to go I didn't have enough money to fly home, so I had to stay. I picked myself up and made as much effort as I could to talk to people and make the most out of my last couple of evenings I had left.

We walked around the back streets to understand the true Barcelona while trying not to get lost.

The last couple of evenings I let my hair down and I spent some of it with the tutors and a few of the students. We went out to an Irish bar and I finished the last evenings off very drunk. I didn't know they just filled a glass up with vodka and coloured it with a shot of orange juice. I'm glad I don't get hangovers that's for sure! I couldn't wait to get back home, even though I had enjoyed the place it would have been nice to have better company.

Back at college that friendship as far as I was concerned was over, but it didn't stop her wanting to be all friendly again when we got home.

MAXINE'S THOUGHTS AND TIPS

What an experience that was, Barcelona is an amazing place and I would love to go back there one day. I found it very lonely on my own out there being my first time abroad, not knowing the language and only eighteen. I was scared, fed up and wasn't very happy with a so-called friend. I really should have got to know my friend first before I took the leap to go away with her. Luckily, I was with a group of 40 people and it wasn't just us.

However, I wouldn't take back the experience. Some friendships are just not meant to be no matter how much you try. Don't let it knock your confidence, because you can't change people into something that they're not. Selfish people do selfish things because it suits them and their situation. Just carry on doing the thing you do best and that's being you!

I woke up with stomach ache, and not thinking much of it I carried on. The next couple of days my tummy was still niggling me and I didn't know why. So, I changed some of the food I was eating and changed a few daily habits, but this pain was consistent.

Every Thursday we would go to a Clairvoyance evening. I didn't really feel up to it that night, but I thought I would get out and take my mind off my pain. I was sitting in my chair while the medium was on the rostrum.

She was talking to people she had picked out of the audience, there were about fifty people in the room that night. Apart from her voice the room was silent, and I kept fidgeting as the pain was getting worse and I just couldn't get comfortable in my chair.

At the interval I got up to get some water and a searing sensation went through my stomach. I fell to my knees cupping my tummy crying with the pain. It felt like someone had pierced a hot poker through my stomach. The pain was unbearable, and I was laying on the floor in the foetal position but no matter what I did or the different positions I lay in the stabbing pain continued.

Pain killers, hot water bottle and rubbing my tummy were not effective in any way. We got home, and I crawled up the stairs. Half way up I just sobbed, "I can't take the pain anymore" I cried, and the emergency Dr was called out.

"It's not her appendix" the Dr said.
"I want you to go in for a scan tomorrow in the meantime here are some very high painkillers."

I got some sleep and went to the hospital in the morning and had an ultrasound.

"I see something but it's not clear I'm going to have to do an internal" said the sonographer.

"You have cysts all over both your ovaries, they are covered. Every time your ovary releases an egg you are going to get this pain as the cyst bursts and releases poison into your system, so your egg can be released."

As soon as she told me this I had a flash back of what my mum had gone through. But I'm only eighteen, I told her, I'm far too young to have anything like this.

Afterwards I had to wait for the specialist who wanted to see me straight away.

"Miss English sit down, I need to go through everything with you. Due to the number of cysts you have on your ovaries and the past surgery your mother has had with her cysts on her ovaries. I'm afraid to say your ovaries are a ticking time bomb. I know you are very young however, I will put this as plain as I can. If you don't have any children by the time you are twenty-five, I'm afraid children will be out of the question. You have a bad case of Polycystic Ovary Syndrome (PCOS). You're going to be tested every year just to make sure you don't need any surgery and have to go through surgery yourself."

I just sat there, dazed and confused. Why am I going through this and why this young? I thought to myself.

When I got home I looked at my partner and things became different. I sat down and explained to him all I have ever wanted was children, but I wanted to go out to work and enjoy my life first and have kids in my thirties I have just over six years to decide what I want to do.

The biggest problem wasn't that he didn't want any kids.
He was so much older than me and his boys had all grown up and were older than I was, but the fact that he had a vasectomy fourteen years previously.

We had been together for over two years and this was the first time that I didn't know where our relationship was going. We started arguing on many levels. I wanted children and he wasn't prepared to go under the knife again to get it reversed.

I was only a few months away from finishing college and wanted to get a job, so I could start up my own business, and at the time he wasn't working. So, I was told I couldn't get a job because he was going back to college as well for a year.

We were bickering over everything, so we split up for a couple of months, knowing I had nowhere to go, I moved all my stuff into the second bedroom and stayed in there.

Within a few weeks I had met a guy in college and we got on very well started going out and dating. That didn't last long because things became strained when my ex-boyfriend saw how happy I was becoming and that most nights I was going out; and being an eighteen-year-old I was given an ultimatum.

"Either we get back together, or you move out this is not a hotel, why should I have you here if you're with someone else."

That evening I drove to my college guy's house, "we need to talk. I'm sorry, I have no choice I must end everything we have between us, I've been given an ultimatum and there is nothing I can do about it I have nowhere else to go."

I was hurting because we got on so well I didn't want to split up with him. He just looked straight at me with those big puppy dog eyes and I could see the hurt in his eyes, he never said a word to me he just walked away and never spoke to me again, not even in college.

It didn't last long and we were back at each other's throats, not only did I resent him because of the ultimatum he gave me, but also because he wouldn't go and have his vasectomy reversed and because I was getting older and feeling my feet becoming an adult, with my own things that I wanted to do and make my own decisions on where I was going next.

I finished college and I called my parents and moved back in with them as it just wasn't working out. I got back in touch with old friends that I hadn't seen or spoken to in a long time.

One being my old school friend from juniors that moved away at senior school, "about time we caught up" I said to her.

We started hanging out again and she was living with her sister. I would go around there, it was like time had stood still and we hadn't long spoken to each other. But I was worried as she was all skin and bone and looking very unhealthy.

I was concerned so after a few weeks I faced her "What's going on with you?" I asked her.

She was taking drugs for breakfast and lunch and having baked beans for dinner it wasn't doing her any good at all.

"You know how much I hate drugs don't you, you're going to kill yourself if you keep doing this to your body" I shouted at her.

We both had tears in our eyes, she knew it and I knew it that she had to stop and quickly.

She was wasting away, but she was stuck. I had to do something about it otherwise I was going to lose my friend forever, drastic action was needed.

What happened next was hard for me to do, however, I looked at it as a life or death situation. I had to do whatever it took to help my friend.

A week or so had past and I caught up with and old friend from school and found out he was dealing amphetamines. I would go around his house for days at a time and chat. He asked me would I like to try some. I told him it wasn't my thing. But then I had a brain wave.

My best friend was in a bad place and I needed to help get her out of it. I'm not the kind of person that gets addicted to things. I agreed, over the next two weeks we were taking up to ten grams a day each and staying awake for days talking, I called my friend. I told her what I had been high the last couple of weeks, I told her what I was taking and how much of it I was doing daily.

"What are you doing? You don't even like drugs, you're going to kill yourself, you can't carry on down this road" I told her she was right.

"How do think I feel seeing you wasting away in front of my eyes? Even when I tell you my concerns you carry on."

The phone was silent, she cried and promised me that she would stop. I told her if she stops I will stop, or we go down together.

She rang me four days later and said she has finally come off the drugs and she will never go back to them. She also said she was going to move out of her sisters too as it was doing her no-good staying there.

What a relief, my friend was safe, so now I had to tell my friend that I no longer wanted any more of his stuff.

He wasn't very happy, we had an argument and he told me there is no way after the amount of stuff I have taken can I stop just like that. I told him I hadn't been doing it for myself but to get a friend to understand how it feels to be on the other side watching and hearing someone you love destroy themselves.

Me doing what I did was going to be the only way for her to stop what she was doing and realise what she was doing to herself.
That was the last time I touched amphetamine, I stopped that day then and there.

But the story didn't stop there. He decided as I wasn't taking the drugs from him anymore that he would take something from me. He told me he liked me, but I didn't see him that way, I rejected him twice that day, and he took it upon himself to take what he wanted from me and raped me.

I was on my front with him on top of me and my hands behind my back. Unable to move I felt helpless I begged him not to carry on, but he took no notice until he finished.

Laying there feeling sick, ashamed, hurt and betrayed. I felt this huge surge of anger well up inside of me and I turned to him and shouted, "How dare you do that to me," the adrenaline fueled through me like it had done once before.

I was shouting and crying, I couldn't stop shaking. I went to go down the stairs and leave the flat. But the next thing I knew I had pulled the long handrail off the wall, broke it in half with my foot and hit him across the head with it and I ran out the flat and never saw him again.

I sat on a park bench in a daze, I couldn't believe what had just happened. I walked to the nearest chemist and asked the pharmacist for the morning after pill.

MAXINE'S THOUGHTS AND TIPS

Being told at the age of eighteen that I had to have children early in my life or I couldn't have them was devastating. Yes, I knew I always wanted children but I definitely was not thinking about them yet. I wanted to have a career and get some money behind me, find the right man, spend some years together, travel the world and have fun. But all I could think about was having children. Again, my choices were taken away from me. If you are getting any kind of abdominal pain go and see your Doctor it might be something different than a period pain.

Being raped I wasn't going to let this situation stop me moving forward in my life, there was nothing I could do about what had happened. I couldn't let it bring me down, but, I could take it with me to make me stronger. It's one of the worst things that could possibly happen to a woman, man or child. I felt violated, dirty, scared and I had my choice taken away from them. I wasn't about to let him destroy my future and I took it as a learning curve and moved forward. I should have gone to the police, but I just wasn't thinking straight at the time. I just wanted it all to end and for life to carry on.

This is how predators get away with things like this. What I should have been thinking was yes, he did it to me and it's over with but what if it happens to another person? I didn't go and get any counselling for what had happened and I pushed it under the rug hoping it would all go away. I blamed myself because I had spent so much time with him, slept over at his flat and chatted for hours through the night. I was embarrassed to speak up to anyone, worried of what people would say and what they would think of me. But it was my right to say NO.

Many people feel this way. I'm not the only one and this is why rapes and assaults are not reported to the police. It's important to remember that it wasn't your fault. Sexual violence is a crime, no matter who commits it or where it happens. Don't be afraid to get the help you need. NO means NO and no matter how great the day or evening has gone, no matter how far you have gone with that other person, if that other person says stop, that's what you do, there are no excuses to carry on. You hear things like this, far too often; (it's gone too far we can't stop now, but we had a great night, you're spoiling it, getting angry about the word NO or STOP)

Everyone has the right to say NO. There shouldn't be any pressure after the word "STOP" to carry on. There is no reason for them to be angry at the other person.

There is always next time when you BOTH feel like you should move forward together. On the other hand, if a person is going near children that needs to be stopped straight away and reported, there is no excuse for that not to be reported. Children are vulnerable and need looking after, they are our future. Let's protect them every chance that we can.

The Crime Survey for England and Wales for March 2017 to March 2018 showed that the police recorded 150,732 sexual offences. This included rape, sexual assault and sexual activity with children and that's the only ones that have been reported in that year and not the men, woman and children that stay silent. That is 150,732 too many.

If you have ever found yourself in this situation, please do things correctly. Don't do what I did because sweeping it under the carpet doesn't get rid of the hurt or the memories, even twenty years later. You need to go and get the morning after pill, get a pregnancy test, get tested for sexually transmitted diseases and you need to talk to someone who can help you. Your first point of call is the Sexual Assault Referral Centre (SARC) if you don't have one close enough to you go to your Doctor and get an urgent appointment. They will provide the treatment you need, and they can refer you to another service if you need more specialist help.

Do not wash yourself or your clothes, this is so forensics can collect DNA from you. These can be collected in the form of blood, saliva, sweat, urine, skin tissue, fingerprints, your fingernails and semen. That's why it's important not to have a bath, shower or wash your hands or to clean your fingernails. Also try not to urinate either until after a sexual assault forensic exam has checked you over as DNA will be washed away. However, they need to check you over within 72 hours, earlier the better.

CHAPTER 6
BEING BRAVE AND GOING IT ALONE

I finally finished my three years at college. Intermediate Art & Design and a BTEC National Diploma in Photography and computer design.

I didn't tell anyone until I finished college that I had applied for a Photography and Media studies course at Nottingham Trent University.

My dream was to travel the world, taking pictures of other countries cultures and this course did this for six months in year two.

I was so excited to be going on this course, but I had to wait. There were only eight spaces available, so I knew it was going to be tight if I got in or not. Weeks had gone past and I'd heard nothing, then I got the letter.

I took the letter upstairs to read it alone just, so I could take my time and see what the news was.

The first thing I see on the letter was "Congratulations you have been accepted into Nottingham Trent University". I was over the moon and so excited that I run down stairs and started dancing around the living room. I waited for both my parents to be in and told them I had something to tell them.

"Mum, Dad guess what…… I got accepted into university".

They both sat there in shock as I hadn't told them that I'd even applied.

Once I had finished bouncing off the walls they sat me down and asked me everything about the course. I explained to them that it was a Photography and Media course.

The first year was more about photography and videoing to learn all the basic skills required. Year two was traveling around Africa, India and Europe for six months taking pictures and learning about diverse cultures, exactly what I always wanted to do. Year three was about developing all the pictures that had been taken as digital cameras had only just come out, and it was going to be all film-based photography. I would be developing all my own negatives and pictures either in black and white or colour and all the videoing we had taken over that time.I would learn how to edit everything and make my own program about my six-month experience. I was ready and raring to go.

My parents looked upset,

"We didn't think you would want to go to university, so we haven't put anything aside for it.

How much are we talking?"

I told them not to worry and that I would call the University tomorrow and tell them they could give my place to someone else. The course was going to be nearly £30,000 over the three years. A student loans was not option so that was the end of the line for my university degree.

MAXINE'S THOUGHTS AND TIPS

There is a lesson to be learned for everyone here, if University is something you want to do when you leave school then you either need to save for it as much as you can or let your parents know as soon as possible so they are prepared for it.

For parents with children this is for you, it's never too early to start saving. We always think we have more time and we blink and there goes five years, we blink again there is another five years gone. My Mum always told me that as you get older the months and years get shorter and I never believed her. But I do now, it only feels like a couple of years ago that my son started school and now he's in college and going to start driving next year. Time goes so fast prepare for your future and theirs now because you won't know when you may need it.

If you haven't just left college and you don't have any children, this is for you too. Retirement comes far too quickly, so do something about it now before it's too late.

I felt gutted when my parents said they couldn't help me. Student loans weren't around back then where you can pay it off weekly when you earn a wage after you graduated.

I was so looking forward to getting away from everything that had gone on in my life over the last ten years, I wanted to travel the world and find new adventures and start a fresh.

Education is the key to life, gain as much knowledge as you can in everything you do. If you have got to that point in your life where you want to do something, but you can't do it right now because of circumstances, put it in your five-year plan and go back to it. You will also probably find that it wasn't the right time back then and it is now. Or as you get older you might even find it's not really what you wanted after all and you want to do something completely different.

Try not to see the negatives in situations like this because you will end up where you are meant to be anyway no matter what you do.

So, let's go through what I did next.

I wanted to do something different. I wanted to give back to the people that helped my mum with her cancer. If it wasn't for those fantastic doctors and nurses at Southend hospital she wouldn't be with us today. I came up with the Breast Cancer Appeal. I got Dad to collect old furniture on his window cleaning round.

He would talk to all his customers, ask then if there was anything they didn't want, then went around their house and collected it all in his trailer. He got everything from wooden units, TV cabinets, paintings to heated rollers.

A few of us went around shops and collected raffle prizes and then we would talk to everyone we saw to buy raffle tickets. I got a free hall, a free DJ and a Free auctioneer. We held an auction during the day followed by a raffle then a big disco in the evening. It was a brilliant day and evening and we raised over £1,500. Mum, Dad and I went to the hospital and handed them the cheque. They were so happy that they invited the local press to take our pictures for what we had done. After that day I always promised to give back.

What am I going to do now? I said to myself, I suppose I should go and get myself a job. If I start now I will stay there till after Christmas save up as much money as I can to start my own photography business. So I printed out my CV and walked around the shopping centre in search of a job.

Later that day I got a call, they asked if I could come in. I went for the interview and I got a job in a jewellers. I worked, and I saved, and I bought some dark room equipment after a couple of months, so I could develop my own pictures. I saved a bit more and a couple of months later I got my camera. I was really enjoying working at the jewellers, I had made friends with the staff and we would all go out at the weekends together, I enjoyed talking, advising and selling to the customers and looking at all the pretty jewellery. I was like a magpie every time something new came in I had to try it on or buy it.

Soon enough I stopped buying photography equipment and

bought the new jewellery that came in instead. I ended up working at the jewellers for over two years.

While I was working there I met up with an old friend from school, I had liked him for years and so did all the other girls. The problem was the more I was getting to know him, the more of the "bad boy" image came out. I began to see white powder around his nose and then he started offering it to me. Every time he got on it he became aggressive.

Within three months we finished seeing each other, it wasn't going to end well for either of us. Not long after that, I got back with my older ex-boyfriend and I moved back in with him on the condition that we have kids by the time he was fifty, so he only had a couple of years to get everything sorted his end.

Over a year rolled on and still nothing was sorted, I began to get agitated that we were wasting each other's time. I turned twenty-one and I gave him an ultimatum. I was giving up, nothing was going to change so I started buying furniture to give him the encouragement that I was leaving if it wasn't sorted soon. We booked a log cabin at Weymouth for five days to see if we could give it one last try to get on the same page.

Two days before the holiday he walked in the kitchen after an argument and he told me he wasn't going and that we were going to stay at home.

"It's booked and paid for, I'm going", I told him.

I drove 3 hours on my own to Weymouth out of stubbornness. I finally got to the log cabin in the woods where we were meant to be staying, it was amazing, so quiet and peaceful. I could hear the birds singing and the trees rustling. Within hours I could feel the stress disintegrating within me, and it was a fantastic feeling. Something I hadn't felt for a long time. I felt at peace.

I unpacked and took a stroll through the woods, around the fishing lake and then over to see the animals that were on site.

Such a beautiful place, I sat there and took the time I needed to think about my next stage of life. I couldn't keep carrying on like this.

The last few years I had been going around in circles not knowing my next step, but just going back to where I felt safe. But things with us just kept going the same way. I knew that after he let me go on our holiday by myself at the last minute that it was my time to move on. We both knew it, but we were both stuck.

After a couple of days on my own I was getting fed up of having nobody to talk to and nobody to enjoy my time with at this beautiful location. I had seen all the sights I wanted to see, the holiday was becoming lifeless. I had to get myself out there and do something, meet new people.

Perhaps go to the family clubhouse that was on site in the evening and try to meet some new people there. When I got in there It wasn't easy, I was sitting at a table on my own, in the middle of a big room, drinking my drink with everyone around me enjoying themselves with their friends and family, I felt so out of place. But I was proud that I built up the courage to go there.

Every day I would call my boyfriend just to tell him how amazing the holiday was and what he was missing out on. The cabin was fantastic, the setting was amazing I even told him about how nice it was walking along the pure sandy beach by the old town, through the cobbled streets and waking up to squirrels sitting outside my window every morning eating acorns.

What I was really hoping for, was for him to change his mind and come to the cabin for the next two days and we could enjoy the rest of the holiday together, but he didn't. I decided then and there, it was over for good between the both of us, I had to change, my situation had to change. I couldn't expect him to change when he didn't want to. I had to get out of this rut with him and just move out, stay out and move on with my life.

The last two days of the holiday I met up with a family from Lincoln; a Mum, Dad and two boys, they were fifteen and nineteen.

I thought it was better to mix with the family and enjoy my last two days rather than sitting in the cabin alone for the rest of the holiday, so that's what I did.

They invited me to go out with them for the day and we went skiing on the dry ski slope not far from the cabins. I had never been skiing before, so I was hoping not to embarrass myself too much, and after a few wobbles, I got the hang of what the instructor was teaching us, but not after I tried to get up the slope on the moving lift and fell flat on my face several times.

It was a good day and exactly what I needed after a bad few days, we laughed the whole time, mainly at me falling over. I spent the evening in the club house with them too talking about how funny our day was, drinking and laughing.

On the last day the two boys and myself went bowling and roller skating. It had been a while but there was no falling over this time. I did a huge amount of skating as a child. It was the best possible finish to a lonely holiday. I travelled the three-hour journey home thinking about what I was going to do or say when I got home. I got in and just said hello. Nothing else was said because we both knew if we had spoken to each other it would have been an argument. I went straight out and visited my parents' and told them what I wanted to do next. I wanted to move out of his house and get my own place, I was done with everything and the holiday was the last straw.

My parents helped me put my name on the council housing list because I didn't have any money put by to rent anywhere. I began to put everything into place, so when a flat did come up I was ready for it. While waiting for that to happen I moved back to my parents' house.

MAXINE'S THOUGHTS AND TIPS

How many of you have gotten yourself into a situation and then the same situation comes back again and again?

It comes back because you haven't learnt by it. Once you learn you move on and that situation doesn't happen again. Afterwards you will get another situation and the same thing happens again and you learn from it and so on. But with every situation you overcome you have learnt something by it every time.

For example, if you put your bare hand into a thorny bush you're going to get cut so you don't do it again – You learn by your mistake and you use gloves. However, if you didn't learn the first time and you go and put your bare hand in the bush again then you will get cut again, and then again, until you learn not to put your hand in the thorny bush repeatedly.

This is Knowledge, this is learning, this is life and it never stops. These situations are going to take your journey with you every step of the way.

See your life as an assault course and you need to get to the finishing line no matter what. Do you get a third of the way around the course and then sit there at the bottom of a 20ft cargo net and say I can't do this? Or maybe you get to the top of the net and then say you have decided to give up.

You must always keep moving forward to the next obstacle, some are going to be harder than others and every one of them is going to be different. Each obstacle you overcome takes you onto the next step of your journey and then the next until you reach that finishing line.

I knew for the last six years I had been going back and forth, going back to the same situation hoping it would change. The problem is, sometimes we don't account for that other person. In the fact they might not want to change, or they don't have the same goals as you.

I was going through so many changes in my life with my parents, school, college, university and a job and he was the only stable thing I could keep a hold of. But I didn't consider his feelings. He loved me for the person I was and not what I became.

I had grown into a young lady with plenty of character and a strong personality and he didn't know how to handle it. He used to make all the decisions but now I was making my own decisions and doing my own thing and he found that hard. We had grown apart, we wanted different things in life; we both knew it but was afraid to take the next step to achieve what we both wanted without each other.

Three months later I got my council flat, it was quicker than I expected but I was so excited, my first place of my own that I could call home. I went and viewed it.

Yuck, it was dirty and looked like it hadn't been cleaned or painted for the last ten years. It needed everything doing to it. However, I was desperate, living with my parents was ok but I didn't want to push it too far and I thought it was best to leave while we were on good terms.

Dad took time off work and spent the next five weeks with me getting the flat ready for me to live in. We were scraping Artex off the walls, painting walls, ceilings and skirting boards, using a blow torch to scrap layers off the doors so they could be painted nicely, we wall papered in the bedroom and living room, laying carpets and moving furniture in.

Each room had a theme, calming blue in the hallway as I walked through the door, the living room had a Chinese theme with black, gold, cream and a touch of red, including Chinese ornaments and picture frames.

The bedroom was Egyptian, all yellows and oranges with Egyptian pictures and figurines around the room, the kitchen had the feel of Africa with terracotta rag rolled walls and African pictures and masks.

A friend helped me paint over the lime green and lilac bathroom with a lovely sunshine yellow so when I was in the bath it felt like I was on holiday as it was nice and bright, and the room would cheer me up. It was my way of travelling around the world without leaving my flat; now we have Google.

In those five weeks I made peace with my Dad, we got on so well even though we were seeing each other every day, laughing and joking. He was showing me how to do the manual job's, so I knew what I was doing any time I needed something done in a room, we were like best friends. It did make me sad in a way because of all those years we had lost with the bad times. I felt like I was meeting my Dad for the very first time.

Even after everything that had happened in the past, I was still a daddy's girl. All the years we had missed out on for Dad and daughter time, I was sad. However, I was only twenty-two, and I had many days, weeks, months and years to spend with him to make up for it. The time was now to spend with my parents, getting to know them without all the illness, the arguments and the excessive drinking. I was looking forward to what the future would bring.

The flat was finished, and it was about time I had a big party to celebrate. I invited all my friends over for drinks and nibbles. People from college, people from work and friends that I had known for years were all together in one place, MY place.

The evening was filled with drinking, laughing, eating, dancing, playing games and one of the guests had bought his guitar with him and he sang us a Turkish song, it was a night to be remembered.

I was finally in a place I was meant to be. I felt happy and contented.

One of my friends bought a guest from work with him, we had met and spoken a few times before but more in passing. He was joining in with everyone and having a good time. A few people stayed over including my friend's guest and he helped me clear up everything from the night before.

As we cleaned we stood there chatting and getting to know each other over the next few hours, we had that connection. What do I do? Do I go with the flow or ignore it? I had only been living in my flat a week and only come out of a long-term relationship not even six months ago.

I was sceptical, but I just went with the flow and thought things would work themselves out. Every day he would go to work and then come around to mine in the evening it wasn't long, before he was staying over every night.

With him came his toothbrush, socks, a change of clothes for work the next day and before long he had his own drawer. It wasn't like he had moved in, it was more like he just didn't leave. It felt like the most natural thing to do.

His cousin moved into his flat to help with his costs and he stayed living with me. We got on so well it wasn't long before I fell completely in love with him. We would put cute post it notes around the flat for the other to find, he bought me a Nokia 5110 mobile phone just so he could text me to tell me he loved me.

He was funny and smart, good looking and easy to talk to, had a good job and wasn't needy. He bought me little gifts just to say he was thinking of me. I couldn't be happier. Wow I thought to myself I have just found the perfect guy. Every time he would call I would get butterflies and every time I looked into his eyes I would melt.

I wanted to marry this guy, but it had only been a couple of months and we were still in the honeymoon stage, knowing how things change from past experiences I kept my cool.

A few months later he came home and told me his security job at the shop he was working in was closing at the end of the month. He had to find work and quick. He was getting stressed and arguments erupted out of nowhere. I kept quiet knowing he was going through a tough time and ignored it.

Luckily, he was only out of work for a week and he'd found another security job on shift work at an oil refinery. He was over the moon with it, now it was time for things to get back to normal. However, it felt a little strange because after those few weeks of arguing things were never the same. He would nit-pick at silly things, he would be short with me or sit on the laptop for hours and ignore me.

The next few months he would come home tired and fall asleep within half hour of coming through the front door when he was on days, and on nights he would go to bed before I got up in the morning. We were like two ships passing in the night, I put it down to the big change in sleep patterns and tried to ignore it and carry on as normal.

Later that year Mum went back into hospital. This time to rebuild her breast that she had taken away after her breast cancer when I was fifteen. There is quite a bit to do in this procedure, they said.

"We are going to take a part of your muscle from your back and put it into your breast so you have some muscle there which will be a great foundation for the implant to rest on top of, once closed we will attach a nipple on the top to make it look as real as possible."

Mum didn't take too well to the operation and her heart stopped on the table twice and they had to revive her. Once she got out of the operating theatre and came back onto the ward, we were told what had happened with her heart.

"Don't tell Mum, she needs all her strength to get better" Dad said.

It was my twenty-second birthday and Mum was still in hospital and I went for a visit. It was nice to see her sitting up in bed awake and bright eyed. I will never forget the present she bought me for my birthday, a battery powered food mixer.

Dad and I looked at each other and laughed. Dad had a few words to say to her about that present, it was the thought that counted. Thanks Mum. I've got something for you too. Here is a clear quartz crystal and I put it into her hand, I looked into her eyes and I said to her

"I promise you from this day on you will never get cancer again, this crystal will cleanse you and keep you clean of cancer."

MAXINE'S THOUGHTS AND TIPS

There she was laying in her hospital bed after another major operation and she's still thinking of me on my birthday, a one in a million mum. Love You Always. That promise is still true to this day.

That wasn't the end of her problems.

There were so many complications that her recovery over the next few months was long and hard. The nipple that was attached got an infection and had to be taken off again and they caught it just in time before she would have lost her whole breast again due to the infection.

Where they took the muscle out of her back, her body wasn't fixing back together again and under the skin was a big deep hole that was too large, and it kept filling up with fluid that had to be drained every month and it would come out either yellow, green or brown.

This mum of mine is a survivor, a heart of gold but tough as old boots. I just hoped this was the end to all her hospital stays and illnesses. She looked tired and you could see in her face she has had enough of being ill, all these operations and hospital stays spanning over twelve years had taken their toll on her body, emotions and confidence.

With me going back and forth to the hospital our relationship wasn't getting any easier because we weren't hardly seeing each other at all. I tried to sit down with him and talk but he was distant, emotionless and not wanting to talk to me. I sat there in front of him and just cried. I told him how I felt about us, and that since he had taken the new job our relationship was suffering, and I cried about my Mum, everything was getting on top of me and I just needed him there right now. We sat, we talked and we resolved some issues, and everything was back on track; or so, I thought…

A few days later I was clearing the flat and his work bag was open in the bedroom. There sitting on top of the bag was a mobile phone box. Why would he need another mobile phone he has one?
I said nothing, but I knew deep down something wasn't right, I ignored the alarm bells and carried on.

The next couple of weeks everything was fine between us, but I still had that niggle in the back on my mind about that phone. So, while he was asleep I looked through his bag. I found the phone, it had a passcode on it. I tried it twice and I couldn't get in, so I left it till the next day after he had used it and tried another two passwords no success. I did this for nine days until I cracked it. OMG!

My heart was pounding, I felt sick to my stomach, I was shaking. Not just because I had cracked it but because I was going through his phone to start with and I felt dishonest and out of order, but I needed to get rid of this gut feeling I had.

I searched through his messages, I looked at his call logs and I just sat there in the bathroom crying.

Trying to be quiet so I didn't wake him up, there was over thirty calls to a couple of girls around 10.30pm and he would stop calling them around 2am and this was every time he was on nights and some calls lasted two hours.

I was so angry; all this time he was on the phone to these girls he could have been ringing me for a two-hour conversation. The call logs said it had been happening for around three weeks, the time I was going back and forth to my mum in the hospital. I couldn't believe what I was seeing.

The messages were to six girls, so I read them all. He hadn't met any of them, so I was slightly relieved. They say your blinded by love and I really was. I put the phone back in his bag and said nothing until I could find the right time and the right words to deal with it.

MAXINE'S THOUGHTS AND TIPS

I hear you all shouting at me while reading this. Pack his bags, tell him to leave, wake him up and kick him out. But, with everything I was going through with my Mum at the time, I couldn't deal with two major issues at the same time. He was my outlet when I needed to talk so it was easier to just leave it.

I'm not saying what I did or didn't do, was right or wrong, but it was the best thing for me right at that time. Mum was still recovering so I was back and forth helping Dad, I was looking at changing jobs, so money would have been an issue too.

The moral to this story is only take on what you can cope with right now. Don't over stretch yourself for the sake of it. At this place and time, it was convenience for me not saying something and I also loved him with all my heart. I didn't just want to give up on that. Our relationship wasn't perfect we both needed to put more effort in especially with the shift pattern he had.

If you were in that situation what would you have done? If I'd stormed in there straight away, that would have been the end of our relationship and I just wasn't ready for that. But then I got thinking why would he bring the box home if it was delivered at work? Did he want me to find it? Did he want me to throw him out, so he could move on with his life or was it him crying out and saying I'm going to start doing this with others if we don't start having a proper relationship? I had to find out. I had to be calm and get all the information I needed.

What I will say is this. Always follow your gut, intuition is there for a reason, so take notice of it.

I decided to make more of an effort so when he was on nights I would go and visit him at work.

Being in security there was nobody around, once an hour he would have to walk around the area which took all of five minutes. I would sit with him talking from about 11pm till 3am.

It wasn't just for the reason for me to make more of an effort, but it was also to spend more time with him and while I was there, he couldn't call the girls on the phone. If he hadn't told them he had a girlfriend they would want to know why he wasn't calling them, get bored and move on.

After a week of visiting him every night I checked his phone there was success, they had both got the hump with him and told him they weren't interested anymore. I was satisfied that I had worked my magic. But because we had spent some time together it bought us closer together again.

We started going out, meeting up with friends, going out for meals. He would talk to me for hours over the phone while he was at work like it was old times again.

A couple of months went by and he began to become distant again. New alarm bells started ringing. My gut was going again, and I needed to find out why. He had been spending a lot of time in the bedroom when he wasn't sleeping. He was asleep on the sofa in the living room. I was awake when he got home from work one morning but kept my eyes closed. I waited an hour to make my move. I crept around the bedroom, so he didn't hear me from the other room. I was searching in all the places I could think of for something, but I didn't know what, however I knew it would be the right thing when I saw it.

Tucked at the back on the wardrobe behind everything was a box folder, it was heavy. I took it out and opened it up, and wow I couldn't believe my eyes. I had found at least a seven hundred pieces of A4 paper with emails back and forth from my boyfriend and twenty-six girls that he was speaking to online.

All their conversations that they had over the last three weeks. He had printed them all out because he couldn't keep up with what lies he was telling each of them and these were his records to keep track. I couldn't believe my eyes, why would he do this to me again? Print them out and bring them home.

This time I wasn't sad I was angry, so I stepped it up a notch. I wrote down every name and phone number I could find and over the space of a week I had read every single email from each of the twenty-six girls.

One was in South Carolina USA, but she was going to fly to the UK to see him. Others he was looking up train ticket prices and dates to go and visit them. So, I stepped into action. While he was in bed I rang every single girl on my list and any new ones that had appeared in the box over a couple of weeks. I told them about me and that we lived together and that I had read all their emails that were between him and them. I wasn't angry with them, it was his fault, none of them knew about me and most of them thanked me for calling them.

When he woke up I couldn't help but make snide comments to him. I wanted him to know but for him to squirm at the same time. He assumed that I had woken up on the wrong side of the bed and wanted to cuddle me, but I didn't want him to even touch me, I was disgusted by what he had done. I was so angry with him. I turned around and said, "I'm going out and I will leave you to talk to all your girlfriends" and I walked out the door. I wondered if he had caught on that I had seen everything.

About four hours later I got back home, and I wanted to know if he had cottoned on to what I said. I went to the bin shed and looked in the big commercial bins out the front of the flat. All black sacks except one bag of paperwork. I picked out the bag and looked inside. It was all the emails. He knew that I knew, there was no going back now. I took all the paper out the bag and walked up three flights of stairs. I could feel the anger filling up inside of me like a volcano, but I had to try and contain myself.I walked in and he offered me a cup of tea.

He was acting like nothing was wrong. He went to walk out the living room and I pushed him back onto the sofa. Got all his paperwork and threw it in his face

"I don't know why you went to so much trouble to get rid of all these, I've been reading them over the last couple of weeks, I've seen all of them" I said to him.

He didn't say a word to me. He just sat there with his head down.

"Why" I asked
"I don't know I was just bored at work so I would look on the internet and chat with people and then it just got out of hand" he said
"Well it's not the first time either is it? I see all your messages on your mobile from the previous time too, oh and every girl you

had on these pieces of paper know all about us because I've rung every one of them and they have been told that you have got a girlfriend and you have been playing them. Now get all your things and leave my flat I don't ever want to see you again!"

MAXINE'S THOUGHTS AND TIPS

You will be surprised what lengths a woman will go to, to find out the truth. We become investigators and sly ninjas. Because we are woman some of you men don't understand that us women pick up on everything. We know your little routines you do, how you act over certain things and any emotional changes and behaviours you have.

There isn't much that gets past a woman's intuition, it just depends whether we tell you or not.

The problem is people always think the grass is greener on the other side but if you're not watering your own grass it's going to be. Make the effort every day to be with the one you love, not just physically but emotionally as well. Life is like an empty jar and if you don't put anything into it, it stays empty. But if you both put something in there every day your life and relationship would be full just like the glass.

Don't ever take for granted what you have got because you won't know what you have lost until its gone.

CHAPTER 7
BABY STEPS

So here I was, beginning a whole new chapter in my life; this really was going to be the first time on my own. Life was going great, I started going out more with the girls, I got myself a new job changing over peoples Gas, Electric and Telephone, which gave me a basic salary plus commission which helped with money.

Until bam it caught me off guard, all the feelings and emotions hit me at the same time. I would sit there at home after work and look at pictures of us together. I missed him so much that my heart ached. I couldn't stop crying for hours.

Work was being affected as I was walking around in a daze, I was missing my weekly targets and once I got in after work I would just sit there and stare into thin air for hours.

Three weeks had gone by and he hadn't called or text me. I couldn't sit by anymore and cry myself to sleep every night I had to do something about it. So, I text him, hi, how you doing?

An agonizing hour later he texts me back. I was like old times we were texting back and forth for the next couple of days. Then he finally asked me to come over to his flat, so he could cook me dinner. My head was screaming no at me, you're a mug, what are you doing? Are you mad? Look at what he has done to you in the past, it's only going to happen again, keep away. But my heart was smiling and dancing, I couldn't stop smiling. I was so excited. Fingers crossed, I said to myself.

He apologised for what he did and said I'd done the right thing by kicking him out, he deserved it.

"Well at least we agree on something", I said to him in jest.

Over the next couple of weeks, we would visit each other's flats. It was a little weird with him sitting in my living room with his jacket on as he had lived there before. I told him that I missed him and still loved him, and that what he'd done had hurt me repeatedly. We talked for hours like when we first met, and all the feelings came rushing back to me. I couldn't help but think of all the fantastic things we had done together in our relationship. He made me a promise that if I would give him a second chance, he would behave himself.

We also made the agreement that we needed to go back to basics within our relationship. We needed space from each other, we thought it would be best if we lived apart for now and then we that would see only the good side of each other and not the grumpy bear in the morning scenario, we needed to take things slowly again. But he insisted that I had a key to his flat.

Let yourself in anytime he said this is a way of me saying I'm committed to just you. So, I took the key.

Over the next few weeks things between us were better that ever. I would stay over his place a couple of times a week and he would spend the night at mine. Because we had our own space, and we could still go and do our own thing, it was working perfectly.

He still had a few things at my flat that I was slowly taking back to his place in the evening. It felt like I was moving him out slowly in my life still, getting used to the fact he was living back a his and not at mine anymore. This was helping me come to terms with him not being there.

A bright Sunday morning I woke up to him saying I needed to leave the flat because he was meeting his friend at London and he was leaving in 30 minutes to catch the train. Begrudgingly I got out of bed, said my goodbyes and left. Everything seemed back on track. I walked down the eight flights of stairs because it took me longer than the lift. I got to my car in the car park and got in. I gave him a quick call,

"Just a quick call! Did you still want to come around mine for dinner later at 6pm?" I said.

"Of course, I will be there" he said.

Sitting there in the car park I got this niggling feeling, something wasn't quite right. Going to London for the day to meet a friend but going to be back at mine for dinner at 6pm. I would have said no if it was me just in case I couldn't make it, especially if it was a friend that I hadn't seen for years.

I sat in the car park for another thirty minutes and he hadn't walked out the flats. It was strange, he got me out the flat asap and he still hadn't left the flat to get the train. Alarm bells were ringing, was he lying to me again? Why did he want me to leave? Should I call him? All these things were rolling around in my head.

I thought I would leave it, and not rock the boat. I spent the day at home and I waited for him to turn up for dinner. There was no sign of him at 6pm so at 6.30pm I called him to tell him his dinner was ready. He apologised and said he had popped home first and he will be round about 7pm. I put his dinner in the oven to keep warm. Then 7pm came and went. I don't know to this day why I did this, but I did. I rang my parents

"Hi Mum, are you and Dad busy? No? great can you meet me at his flat car park please. I have some extra things I want to take there but I can't carry them all up at once and it saves me taking three trips".

My parents got there and I gave Mum a stool, Dad some folders of paperwork and I had a small box. They knew that it was an excuse to get them round as I could have taken these things anytime.

We got to the fourth floor, walked to his flat, I put my key in the door and opened it. There he was in his living room painting, and there was his ex-girlfriend laying in his bed, the one that I had crawled out of ten hours ago sitting there watching TV in his jumper.

The look of surprise on his face was a picture.

"What the hell are you doing?" I asked him.

He explained his lame story to me. He said he was meant to be going to London to meet his friend but just after I left the flat his "ex-girlfriend" text saying she needed help and wanted to talk so she came to visit him from London and it was too late for her to leave as it was too dark for her to walk around London on her own so late at night, and they weren't doing anything, apparently.

From that moment everything turned from bad to worse. I threw his stuff at him. I was so angry because he had let me down again. We were arguing and shouting at each other, and then from the bed I heard

"Why don't you get out of here?"

I couldn't believe that came out of her mouth. I looked at her and I just saw red. Up until that moment I had forgotten she was even there. I jumped on the bed and just kicked her in the face.

"How dare you tell me to get out" I told her while pinning her to the bed and punching her.I couldn't stop. Mum was shouting at me to get off her. My man tried grabbing me as he knew she had no chance of getting away, which made me even more angry that he was defending her.

Dad went for him and pinned him against the wall while telling him not to touch me and that she deserves everything she gets, the next thing there was this almighty crash.

Dad had thrown a large old-fashioned TV at the wall just missing his head. I stopped, got up and pulled Dad off him, and she ran off out the flat. I chased after her. Within a few minutes I had come to my senses and stopped. If only she had just sat there and said nothing, we wouldn't be in this mess right now.

I walked back up to the flat, no one was there. I had to find out if everything was planned out from the start. I didn't believe him at all, but I needed the evidence to back that up. I found her rucksack and emptied the contents onto the floor of the bedroom. Her phone was in there, but it was locked. However, there was also a toothbrush and a change of clothes in there too.

I sat there and cried, I was so angry that he then lied to my face again. I took her clean bra and knickers and left the flat, ripping them as I walked down the stairs.

I found his car and tied them around his window screen wipers and wing mirrors just to let him know that I had found them and that I knew he was lying.

The next morning there was a knock at the door and two policemen stood in the doorway.

"There was an incident last night and we have come to take you down to the station to get a statement from you"

She had gotten me arrested for hitting her and breaking her glasses and he had taken her to the police station. They took my DNA and my finger prints, took my statement of what happened, and they let me go with a caution.

Unbeknown to me, her Dad was a police officer and he wasn't letting it lay to rest that his little girl had been hit. That was it, I'd had enough of him and his cheating ways and we didn't speak or see each other again. I didn't learn, after everything that had happened three weeks later he came back with his tail between his legs and apologised to me for what had happened.

I told him I felt let down after all the promises he had made and all he did was go back on all of them. I told him I loved him so much, but he had broken my heart so many times, I couldn't handle it again.

However, your heart wants what your heart wants. I knew I wanted him in my life. After many lengthy discussions we decided that it was best if we weren't together but remained good friends.

The next couple of months were troublesome free we were getting on great as friends, everything was good. So, I mentioned about us going away together and just having a break and a laugh. Getting out from the same four walls we both agreed it was a great idea.

I booked a few days away to Norfolk in a caravan, we had a great time out on the town, bowling, crazy golf, go karting and even crabbing.

We had so much fun that our eyes met for the first time in months and we knew what each other was thinking and we were both on the same wavelength. We had such a good time and all the feelings were there. But we carried on as friends.

On the way back, we stopped off at my parent's caravan and ended up staying for the whole weekend. Dad welcomed him with open arms, but my Mum wasn't so sure.

You see my dad was a street fighter back in the 60's and 70's, where you punch first and ask questions later, buy the guy a pint and by the end of the night you were best mates.

We had a fantastic weekend of laughing and drinking between the four of us, it couldn't have gone any better. Friday evening it was perfect to walk along the beach, it had been a warm day, the sun was going down over the water.

The sky was filled with beautiful colours; yellows and orange. He told me how he felt about me, and I felt the same. We cleared the air and we decided to give it one last go with 100% effort on both parts. He knew he had to grow up and stop acting like a teenager and being scared to settle. Neither of us wanted to give up on each other, we just needed to change what we were doing. The problem was he used to be in the British Army as a Royal Signaller. He lived and travelled all over the world and was involved with war overseas.

One of the reasons why he came out was because of his mental health. He couldn't get over seeing babies and children suffering and dying every day. It had messed with his head and every time he got close to someone he would go into self-destruct mode and destroy everything around him. So, I felt inclined to give him the extra leeway, so he could come off the Prozac and move forward.

Once we had got back from holiday everything was still going amazingly. He wanted to change his job but there wasn't much out there, so we just tried our best with what we had.

Within a couple of weeks, I started getting stomach aches and I would bloat right out after certain foods I was eating. I went to the doctors to go and get everything checked out. She ran a few tests and told me to ring back in ten days. It was only six days later, and I got a call from the doctor's receptionist.

"Your results have come back early, and I want to say congratulations, you're pregnant. We need to book you in for a scan."

I couldn't believe what I was hearing, we had discussed children however, we weren't trying for a baby and we had only been back together for a few weeks. I didn't know whether to panic, be overjoyed or scared. I think I was feeling all three of them.

Because I had the PCOS I didn't have regular periods so any time I didn't have a period I didn't think anything of it. It was a complete surprise especially as I was on the pill too, but I had missed a couple out.

I rang my boyfriend and I told him that I'd got my tests back early. He was concerned that there was something wrong.

"Nope nothing wrong, I'm all ok."
"Well that's good then, so when am I going to be a father?" he sniggered on the other end of the phone
"In about nine months", I told him.

The phone went silent. It wasn't the way I wanted to tell him. I would of rather it had been face to face but it just came out. He was in shock and he wasn't expecting that answer. He got home that evening and gave me a big cuddle.

What a relief, it could have gone completely the other way. We had our appointment at the hospital to get an ultrasound so we could see how far along I was and so we could we see our baby for the first time. We got to the hospital and we were called in.

The sonographer put cold gel on my tummy with the probe and checked her screen for measurements of the baby and to see how far along I was. I didn't understand what she was looking at with the black and white grainy images. We asked her a lot of questions and she showed us what we were looking at. It didn't look like a baby it was more like a peanut. We were told I was only 5 weeks pregnant and I would need to book in for a twelve-week scan. We counted back and worked it out I got pregnant a week after the holiday.

We wanted to do the right thing, so he moved back in my flat. We talked about selling his flat to pay off all his debts and for us to have a fresh start in our new life together as a family.

At twelve weeks we went back to the hospital and had our first proper scan where they check everything is ok. We got in the hospital and saw our baby growing inside of me. It was a magical moment, there was no longer a peanut, but a baby. Until this moment it didn't feel real but now we could see the head, arms and legs forming. I fell in love straight away.

On the way home, my boyfriend was quiet. I asked him what was up with him. He said there was nothing wrong, but I knew different.

We got home he told me that he didn't want the baby to have his last name. I was shocked and hurt. We had an argument; my emotions were running high right now. Insecurities were setting in that he didn't want this baby and that he was going to leave me on my own with a new-born.

MAXINE'S THOUGHTS AND TIPS

There are no excuses when someone treats you bad, cheats and lies to you. "You are worth so much more than this", I used to tell myself, then I would turn around and say "yeah but I love him" I made it acceptable. My love for him was blinding me, I couldn't see the real him and when I did, I just told myself I was overreacting. While he was going through his depression, I was giving him the ok to do it more because I wasn't nipping it in the bud and stopping it. I was telling him I was happy to accept his bad behaviour by taking him back every time.

I wasn't telling him that I'm worth more than how he was treating me. I should have never kept taking him back, but I did. I was holding on to him tightly. Even though I had my own flat but, I was on my own for the first time and I was afraid of being alone. I was lonely, and I was now going around in circles again like I did in the last long-term relationship.

Do you know why I was going around in circles? I do!

Because I didn't learn from it the first-time round. Only in the last relationship our arguments were about me wanting to have children. This relationship our arguments were about me having a child. This time I had everything I wanted in life. I got what I asked for. However, I still didn't get what I wanted.

Be careful what you wish for, you may just get it. But not as you thought you would.

By the time four months came around I was getting morning sickness all through the day, but I still had to go out to work, walking the streets door to door changing people's gas, electric and telephone.

I was getting tired of walking the streets for eight hours a day, my legs were swollen, my feet hurt with all the extra weight and to top it off it was snowing, and I was so big I couldn't get my jacket zipped up. I was trying so hard to save up money, so we could leave the flat when the baby was born.

The problem was I had come out of a two-bedroom house and my flat had just the right number of items in there for the space, however when my boyfriend moved in fully with all his stuff we stacked it all in the bedroom. The only space there was in that room was a walkway to the chest of draws and wardrobe, the rest of the room was full to the ceiling of boxes and furniture.

We slept, ate, entertained guests and chilled out all in the living room. Once we pulled the futon out there was hardly enough room to walk around. We had to seriously think about where we were going to put our baby; we had no room. We already had a futon bed, computer table and chair, Stereo unit, TV stand, Bookcase and now we needed a space for the cot. It wasn't working out so well and it was causing more arguments.

We were both feeling a little trapped and enclosed. He suggested about moving into his flat, it had two bedrooms, so it made sense.

However, with the uneasiness about what had happened in the past, I wasn't giving up my council flat for him to throw me out with a baby if things went pear shaped. We just had to make do.

My twenty-week scan was here, wow it had come around so fast. Half way through already, but it was an exciting day. Today was the day we found out what our baby was. Casey for a girl and either Brandon or Ryan for a boy.

We got to the hospital and I was so excited I felt like I could burst. We sat there for ages in the waiting room then we got called in. The same as before with the gel and the probe but wow we really could see our little precious.

We could see the tiny fingers and toes, long legs and big feet, and it had hiccups, we could hear the amazing heartbeat and every time she put the probe on my belly the baby kicked it off again it was all very cute. Everything is perfect she said, and your due date is 7th May 2002.

"Well what are we having?" we asked her.
"You have a little BOY", she said.
Oh, wow amazing, now we could go and get a few more things bought and sorted ready for the delivery.

On the way home, my boyfriend was beaming. "Now I know it's going to be a boy, I want the baby in my name" he said.

"What! Now you know it's a boy you want him in your name but if it was a girl you wouldn't?"
"Well he can carry my name on she couldn't", he said.

I told him point blank there and then that if he wants to have the baby in his name then he will have to marry me first or suck it up that the baby will have my last name.

This argument went on for weeks and I wouldn't back down, how dare he turn around and tell me he didn't want the baby in his name, then say he did only because it's a boy. It wasn't going to happen.

Two weeks after my scan I got a call from my Dad, and he told me that Mum had been rushed to hospital thirty minutes ago.
She had a stroke. I felt the life drain out of me and we rushed to the hospital. We weren't allowed to see her straight away, they had to do tests and keep her in to see how she was in the morning.

Luckily the ambulance had got to her quick enough and she was recovering. She had lost most of the use in her arm and leg. Her speech was slurred which got better over the days to follow. She told me she was giving up. But it wasn't her time, she had a grandson to help me with. She got to work with the physiotherapist who was working on her arm and leg daily.

Three long weeks later she walked out of hospital.

<u>MAXINE'S THOUGHTS AND TIPS</u>

I was ecstatic to find out I was having a baby boy, then again, I would have been ecstatic if it was a girl, if the baby was healthy that's what mattered. But some people including my boyfriend wanted it to be a boy and thought more of the baby because of it and that really annoyed me.

Babies are babies no matter what sex they are. Girls are just as important as boys it shouldn't make a difference in this day and age. There is no need to love a baby less just because it's not the gender you wanted. Anyone with a child should think themselves lucky. There are thousands of women out there who would love to be even able to carry a baby. Or men who can't have their own children.

However, we also must look at the core of the problem. Men don't go through nine and a half months of carrying a child, feeling the most amazing movements inside of them, hearing another heartbeat coming out of their own body. So, most, if not all women accept their child no matter what sex it is. In my opinion with men it comes down to two things.

1. The way they were bought up and how their own Father thought about genders
2. Because they are boys it's a scary thought to bring a daughter into the world and bring her up. Not knowing what she likes or doesn't like. Her thoughts and feelings and different rates of maturity. It can be scary for some men.

My Dad had that issue that he found it harder to bring me up than all his son's put together. And told me often, normally when I was getting told off. Any time we spent together was when we were painting, stripping a car or woodwork; he didn't know how to handle a girl.

Stroke symptoms:
The main symptoms of stroke can be remembered with the word F.A.S.T.:

- Face – the face may have dropped on one side and may not be able to smile. Their eye or mouth may have dropped.
- Arms – the person may not be able to lift both arms and keep them up. There may be a weakness or numbness in one of their arms.
- Speech – their speech may be slurred or garbled, or the person may not be able to talk at all even though they are awake.
- Time – dial 999 immediately if you see any of these signs or symptoms, time is off the essence.

There are two main causes of strokes:

- ischemic – a blood clot stops the supply of blood, this is what happens in most cases
- hemorrhagic – a weakened blood vessel supplying the brain bursts

A related condition known as a transient ischemic attack (TIA), where the blood supply to the brain is temporarily interrupted - known as a mini-stroke which lasts between a few minutes and several hours.

These conditions increase the risk of having a stroke:

- high blood pressure (hypertension)
- high cholesterol
- atrial fibrillation
- diabetes

If you are, or someone you know is having any signs don't hesitate, get yourself or them checked out. It's not a nice thing to go through or to watch someone else go through, and not be able to help them. Mum said she was just standing there doing a crossword puzzle then suddenly, she collapsed on the floor and she couldn't move. It's that quick.

Later we found she had high cholesterol and she never knew. So, look after yourself.

With Mum being the best, she could be, I was still going back and forth to see her, working full time in the freezing cold. I was feeling emotional, tired and drained. But I knew I had to keep moving forward.

I was seven months pregnant.

I got home early one day, I'd had enough at work for the day and I caught him chatting up women online again. We got into a big argument about me not being at home so much and that he felt so lonely. I shouted at him to stop being so selfish, that it wasn't all about him. I was dealing with Mum, working full time and being pregnant. He walked out the door and slammed it behind him.

Because I was pregnant and didn't just have me to protect from his lying and cheating ways, I had to protect the future of our baby. I found each girls number on his phone he was talking to and called them. I told them I was seven months pregnant with his baby and that he'd lied to them all. They were disgusted with him and so was I. He got a few nasty texts back saying never to call them again. He came back, and I told him I had called them.
I faced him with it. He got angry and threw my phone at my head and broke it. I picked the phone up and threw it back at him, hitting the front door behind him. He came for me and pinned me up against the wall by my throat and kneed me in the stomach. I went into complete protective Mother mode, I just saw red pushed him off me and punched him on the nose and chucked him out.

I phoned my Dad and told him what had happened.

"Don't make rash decisions" he said.

I couldn't believe what I was hearing. I was shouting at him down the phone that he was letting me down saying that it was ok for me to be treated like that.

A couple of days later my dad and my boyfriend came around to talk to me. Dad was saying it wasn't about us two anymore it was about the baby that's coming into the world and he didn't ask for his parents to be at each other throats.

"Think of him" he said.

My boyfriend apologized for his behaviour and Dad threatened him with being six foot under if he touched me again. We put it behind us and carried on being together, but things were not the same after that, I had closed off that part of my heart from him and he knew it. We were carrying on for the sake of the baby. We did our own thing.

He would sit at home on his day off and play his computer games or chatting women up online which he printed out and left around the flat. I was alone and unhappy and about to start my life as a single parent; it's not how I wanted things to be but there was nothing I could do.

With not long until the baby was born I found a place for the cot to go. The futon had to stay down to make life easier as it was too heavy for me.

Once all the baby stuff was bought and, in the room, and everything was set up, there was a 2ft square of space in the middle of the room and that was it. We needed to get out of here, this place was far too small for the three of us and he wasn't even born yet. We sat down and discussed our relationship and the future. I knew I was going to have to bring this baby up alone, but we agreed that he would stay until the council gave us a bigger place to live.

It was the 19th May 2002 and my baby boy was nowhere to be seen. I had to go in and be induced. I was so scared of what was going to happen next. My boyfriend came with me and we sat there and talked for a few hours. At 8pm that evening I was induced.

To my horror they told him to go home, he wasn't allowed to stay. Being my first time, I didn't know what to expect I was so scared.

At 11pm the pain started, I was given paracetamol and within the next hour I was given gas and air to numb the contraction pains. At 2am I was given pethidine in the muscle in my leg wow! that was painful and did nothing for the pain. I was up all night with contractions. I called my boyfriend at 5.30am and told him he needed to come in right away, and to call my parents and bring them too.

By 6am I was 5cm dilated and transported into the delivery room. The pain was getting unbearable and an epidural was the next drug on my list. I was in so much pain that my body was tense, and it was stopping the dilation. I needed to relax. I'd had so much gas as air I kept falling asleep, so they took it away from me.

The gas and air had made my mouth so dry that I couldn't stop drinking. I'd drank a litre of water, now because my bladder was full the baby wouldn't come out so they had to empty it as I wasn't allowed to go to the bathroom, so I had to have a catheter fitted to drain the fluid build-up which was also very painful.

I wasn't enjoying child birth at all, the feeling of a baby inside was an amazing experience but this was not. A second epidural was given, I was numb down my legs and on my belly but not where I was meant to be numb.

After all the pain medication my body was not going to get to 10cm dilated. The doctor decided to cut me from front to back, so the baby had enough room to come out. Luckily, I couldn't feel the cut, I'm glad the epidural was working by then.

At 12.03pm on 20th May 2002 Ryan was born with help by

suction cup. The doctor had to help him out as he was stuck. I was absolutely shattered. I told the nurses to give him straight to his Dad. I had run out of energy, my Mum was the next to hold him, then my Dad.

Once I had come around from all the drugs I'd had a mummy cuddle. I didn't mind not having the first cuddles I'd been cuddling him for the last 10 months and it was their turn.

It took forty-five minutes to be sewn up, I even made a joke to the doctor and asked if he was going to sign the cross-stitch pattern he had just done.

I was taken up to the ward with baby Ryan. He was so cute, he had these amazing tiny little fingers, long feet with little cute toes. He smelt gorgeous, will always remember the baby smell. His 0-3mth baby grows were so baggy on him around his belly, but length ways he fit them top to toe.

We both had to stay in hospital for eight days. I had an infection and my legs ballooned up so much you could no longer see my toes as my feet were so swollen. I was on 48-hour bed rest. Ryan was in ICU for jaundice and he also had an infection.

I met a lovely new mum whose son was also born on the same day as Ryan was. She had a Caesarean, she had to stay in too and she was in there for seven days, and I was glad of the company.

My boyfriend and I sat together looking at the baby we had produced. We were so contented about our new little family, so much so he told me he didn't want to leave anymore and wanted to stay.

"We are a family and I want to look after you both." He said.

There was one thing standing in the way of a perfect happy ending. It was time to register Ryan. The argument we had when I was pregnant come flooding back, he was going in my name unless we were married, I said and we had a ten-minute argument in the registry office.

CHAPTER 8
UNTIL I SEE YOU AGAIN

Mum and dad said they were happy to help as much as they could, with us being first time parents it was scary looking after a little human.

To make life easier they suggested the three of us go and stay with them for a while. I still had my stitches in and was very sore, my boyfriend was going back to work in a few days, so he couldn't help much. The three of us moved in to my parents' house for a while, until I was back on my feet.

My parents were in their element with seven children between them; they knew everything inside out. They showed us how to bath him, change his nappy, best way to hold and feed him. It was easy enough for me because I had helped with some of my nieces and nephews, but this was his first time in every aspect.

It was time for him to go back to work, he wasn't ready to go back yet but he had no choice. However, once he had gone back to work, he didn't really come around to see us as much once he had finished for the day.

My parents' house was on the way home, so he could have come and seen me and his son for ten minutes every day after work, but he drove past the house and straight home and went to bed.

The more he did that the more I wanted to stay with my parents and not be in an empty cramped flat. It even got to the point that we didn't see him for two weeks.

After two months it was time to move back home. I was so grateful for the help I received from them. I spoke to my boyfriend on my day off. I told him that I now know where his priorities lie and that wasn't with us. He agreed, and we came back to the arrangement of him staying until we got a house.

The Health Visitor would visit us regularly at the flat, she was most upset about how small our flat was and how dangerous it was for a baby to live there, that she wrote a couple of letters to the council explaining that the flat was unsuitable for us and we needed to move as soon as possible.

My parents would call daily to see how we were doing, they were both missing having a baby in the house so when Ryan was four months old I went back to work part time and he went to my parents on my work days until after Christmas when my job finished, as it was only temporary.

Numerous letters were being written to the council to get us moved. The time had finally come, and Ryan was 8 months old when we moved into a 3-bedroom, five-story townhouse about fifteen minutes down the road. The living room was the size of my flat; there was so much space it was great. I expected my boyfriend to leave but he told me he wanted to stay. He wanted to watch Ryan grow and be in his life.

We settled into our new place, four months later Ryan had his first birthday party, we had the space to invite our friends and family. Ryan was enjoying his party of sandwiches, crisps and cake but his dad just didn't seem interested in being there.

Two days later my boyfriend had a first aid course booked with work up North. It was only for a few days, and it was going to be strange as this was the first time Ryan and myself would be alone together, but I was really looking forward to it. I rang him a few hours later to make sure he got to his first aid course, but he was unreachable. Not just that evening but for the whole time he was up there.

The day he came back he was very cagey about the trip, so, I asked him if he went up there to meet a girl from the internet.

He said no, but I could see he was lying to my face, but I couldn't prove it, I had no evidence, I had to take his word for it. I couldn't get it out of my head, so I kept pushing for more information.

He never turned around and said yes he was with a girl, however, he couldn't tell me why he never took his phone out with him, why he didn't answer at any time, he just got angry at me and told me what he got up to in the evening was none of my business and that he was going to leave me guessing.

I knew in my head and my heart what he had done, that phone never leaves his side ever, he was ignoring my calls and meeting this girl from the same town he was having his first aid course, coincidence I think not.

I slapped him round the face and told him to leave.

He took his laptop, one change of clothes, and his coffee maker walked out the door and slammed it behind him.

Later that evening he came back, he had nowhere to go, he was sorry and asked if he could come back. He told me he wouldn't be going up north any more. I couldn't see him on the streets and I had only just gone for a job interview and I was going on a course the week after, so I needed him there.

June 2003, I started my new job in double glazing. I had to go on this course, so my boyfriend took a week off work to look after Ryan. I rang him three times a day to make sure everything was ok, it was the first time he had looked after him on his own since becoming a father.

On the last day we finished the course three hours earlier than expected, so, I came straight home I got there around 4pm. I walked up the stairs to see my little boy, I was so looking forward to seeing him and it was the longest I had been away from him.

When I got to the living room my boyfriend was sitting on the sofa on his laptop eating sweets and Ryan was walking around the living room wining and not knowing what to do with himself. I picked him up to give him a cuddle and he was soaking wet. I didn't even get a hello from him and he was taking no notice of the baby at all. I asked him when was the last time you changed him?

"This morning when we got up" he said.

That was 8-9 hours ago. I then asked him when he last fed him. He said he didn't know, but that he had had a bottle first thing this morning and a biscuit. He told me he had been whining all day.

I hit the roof, I went and made Ryan a bottle of milk. Laid him down to change his bum as it was sagging around his knees. I went and got a clean nappy, a change of clothes and cream. I stripped him down completely and all I saw was my son's concave belly and ribs poking out of his skin, his legs had lost all their rolls, his spine was protruding through his skin in his back. I had been away for five days and he had starved him the whole time I had been gone. I sat there and cried, how could he of down that to his own son. I was so angry with him I wanted to scream but I sat on the floor giving him a big mummy cuddle while drinking his bottle until he fell asleep. I put him upstairs to sleep and get away from what I was about to do.

He was still sitting on the sofa playing his games. I took his laptop and dropped it on the floor.

"You are willing to let your child die of starvation, so you can play your stupid games?" I shouted at him.
I picked my boyfriend up and I threw him across the room.
"Pack a bag and don't ever come back", I told him.

Now I had another problem.

Two weeks previously I had got a loan out. We had sold his flat and all the profit he made of it paid off most of the twenty-one thousand pounds that he owed but he had come up slightly short. He asked me to get a loan out to pay the remainder. We were getting on well and things were looking up and we were making a go of it, so I did.

I got a loan for £5000 and had to repay £7000 so now I was left with a bank loan, being a single parent and having a full-time job that was 80 hours a week with no child care. However, I couldn't give it up work to look after my son due to the bank loan.

I reluctantly told Dad what had happened and the situation I had been left in. He got an appointment with the bank and got a loan. He gave me the money to pay off the loan I'd had and it was at a better rate, then all I had to do was pay Dad every month.

Trying to handle a one year old, work six days a week and getting money together was a struggle. My job was commission only so I couldn't cut my hours down or go part time it just wouldn't have worked. I sat with my parents and explained the situation. I had to put my heart and soul into work, so I could get ahead. So, my parents took care of Ryan every day for me, you might as well say he lived with them for six months as most days I didn't get home from work until 11pm. I would visit him between seeing customers and on my day off, I wanted to bulk pay Dad off as quickly as I could. I felt guilty putting all my effort into work and not being able to be there for my son. I knew it was a means to an end, but I got to the point I was getting depressed with constantly working all the time and not having a life of my own. I would tell myself that Ryan would be better off without me, having a father that left him never to return and a mother that was working all day, every day just to survive the next day, week, month and year.

The guilt was killing me, which in turn, turned into resentment. He walked out from me and his own flesh and blood not having a care in the world to how his son was, not having to buy nappies, spending nights cuddling him or what his needs were every day, keeping a roof over his head. It was crushing me that he no longer cared about either of us and not one single phone call.

I called his parents and explained what had happened between us. He wasn't that close to them but I thought they had the right to know, as it was their grandchild. On the phone I told them they could see him whenever they wanted, however the response I got I didn't expect. They said to me,

"Well now our son has walked out we don't have to see Ryan, you weren't married when he was born so as far as we are concerned, he isn't our grandson, please don't call back again".

I was gob smacked, I sat there on the bed and cried. Ryan had lost a whole side of his family in the space of a few days. The more I thought about it the angrier I got with all of them. The resentment I had that he was out enjoying himself free to do what he wanted whenever he wanted and I was stuck in my life going round and round and feeling like I was getting nowhere fast. I got to the stage that if he could do it then so could I. He was in a warm loving place with my parents.

After work I started going out getting drunk. Sleeping in my car, not going home for days. I pushed myself completely into work. I was doing well, got promoted, and became the top show home consultant of the branch because I was pushing myself, and hiding the pain of everything I was going through.

My work was my escape from the pain I was in, it got to the point I would work on my day off because every time I took time out of work I would look at Ryan or go home and I would cry for hours.

It would bring all the pain of my life flooding back. I had to keep working, I couldn't work if I was crying, so I sat my parents down and asked them if they would adopt my son. It was the hardest thing in the world to do.

I told them that I loved him, but he would have a better life there with them, someone who would hold him and play with him rather than just cry in his presence. Someone who could love him like he deserved to be loved and not have someone feel numb around him. I couldn't give him what he needed.

Mum was so angry, she told me how selfish I was being and that I shouldn't be working at all, my place is to be at home with my son. The argument escalated, and I walked out.

Back at work that day I asked if everyone wanted to go out for the night, it was a school night, but I had to do something to get me out of this mood I was livid, I was trying to get myself out of this hole and all she could think about was her old fashion ways.

The eight of us went out for the night including some of the new people at work. I drowned my sorrows by drinking everything I could get my hands on. I don't remember going around a friend's house that night or how I got there.

But what I do remember is waking up groggy in the morning with a huge hangover and one of the new guys from work behind me finishing himself off inside me, he got up pulled his trousers up and walked out the door before I was completely awake. I felt the wetness run down my leg, the realization come over me what had just happened.

I got up and quietly went into the bathroom. I just looked at myself in the mirror and cried, not again! I pulled myself together sorted myself out and went to the chemist. He never came back to work after that and it was the last time I saw him. However, I did find out that he went back to Nigeria where his pregnant girlfriend was living.

MAXINE'S THOUGHTS AND TIPS

This was one of my most joyous and worst times of my life, I had this beautiful perfect baby that I had always dreamed about but the situation I was in stopped me from seeing that. I knew I was hurting by what he had done to me previously. I was just trying to do everything I could to keep my family together. Even though I loved him with all my heart I couldn't forgive him for what he did to our son. I couldn't stand by and let him do that to him. I had to choose between the two of them. I didn't want to, but I felt I had no choice. I had to do what was right by Ryan.

When he left with his laptop, a change of clothes and his coffee maker, leaving the rest of his life behind, in the back of my mind I felt like he was coming back. He was all over the house and I had kept him there. My heart was breaking and my whole body was numb, I couldn't feel anything for anyone who was close to me including my son. I look back on that time now with much sadness. I feel as though things could have been so much better if only I would have let go of my boyfriend for once and for all.

In hindsight I know I was depressed, and I wasn't coping but I didn't do anything about it. I know now that if things get too much for me I find that I bury myself into work and close the outside world off. I know if I feel like that, I need to stop everything I'm doing, and I re-evaluate what's happening in my life because something isn't right and it's not working so I know I need to change it. I know that about myself now, I see the triggers.

I'm not the kind of person who gets addicted to things, so alcohol was never the issue. My issue was doing the opposite to what I should be doing so I didn't have to think about the guilt, resentment and hurt I was feeling so to put a stop to everything I ignored everything to do with that pain I was in. I became numb because it was easier to cope with. I thought by asking my mum to adopt him I was being unselfish because it's what was best for him.

My parents didn't know the pain I was going through, no one did I hid it very well. All I knew is for my own sanity I couldn't stop what I was doing with work and start feeling because I would fall apart. I knew at some point soon I would have to face it, but that time just wasn't now. The universe would only give me so much time to sort myself out before something was put in place for me to stop me from self-destructing completely.

The rape felt surreal as it was nothing like the first one, I was asleep through it all, even though when I woke up and cried but I didn't act or go to the police because I was numb to that too. I felt nothing about what had happened, I cried because I knew there was something wrong with me because I was numb to it. I was at rock bottom and I needed act now before things got any worse.

128

I needed to change and move forward, I started taking my days off, I would come home early as much as I could and not go out in the evening as much.

Even if stayed at my parents' house and saw him for an hour in the morning at least that was something towards making things right. I knew things needed to change. I tried to turn my life around and get my priorities straight. To be there for my son more, give him the love and affection that he needed while I was still working.

Staying at my parents I noticed Dad rubbing his back and stretching when he thought no one was around. I asked him what was up, he told him that he had back ache the last 3-4 months and it wasn't shifting. We argued that he should go to the doctor but being the stubborn man that he was he wouldn't go. An appointment was made for him. They did some blood tests and some x-rays.

They found that Dad had some marks on his lungs, more tests were taken. The results were back. Dad had Lung Cancer but because it had been left so long it had already started spreading in his lymph nodes and around his body and there was nothing they could do, it was just a matter of time. They still gave him radiotherapy and chemotherapy to see if they could shrink it, but it was a very small chance.

Mum was devastated, I was in shock and I was distraught. I'd only had my Dad for three years, I'd only just found him and now he was going to be taken away from me, I was gutted. Mum went into meltdown. She had gone through two lots of cancer, cysts and a stroke and she was still here.

Dad gets cancer and he is a ticking time bomb.

Repeatedly she would say, "It should have been me to go first".

It was my time again to be strong for them both. They needed me so much. I told Dad I was going to give up work to help them both out and put Ryan into playgroup.

He wasn't very happy about that, he told me how proud he was of me and that I could have just gone onto benefits and been a single mum and done nothing, but I worked hard and did everything I could for my son, I sat there and cried as that was the first time dad had told me he was proud of me and that meant the world.

I told him how I felt about everything that had happened between us, and we cried together. We both knew there and then that he wasn't going to survive this. I promised him that I would look after Ryan and that Mum would be ok and that I would always be there for her no matter what.

He made me promise to never give up on my dreams, to always work hard by going that extra mile and help others in need. "I promise Dad, I will never let you down."

Dad started his treatment. Seeing my dad going from the strongest person I had ever met to not even being able to pick up a glass of water was heart-breaking.

Mum every evening fell to bits so I had to stand strong. I couldn't let either of them down. I had to step up and take the reins to make sure everything didn't fall apart.

Dad pulled me aside,
"I want to give up, I can't take this anymore,
let me die", he told me.

My heart shattered, but I couldn't look weak I had to carry on being strong.

"Dad you have always been strong, and you have carried this family through thick and thin, physically you can't do that anymore, it's now my turn; you just concentrate on yourself.
You can't give up! You need to be here for Mum and Ryan they

need you, I need you". I wasn't ready to let go, I was still building myself up to be the strongest person they needed me to be. But on the outside, I had it aced.

I needed to change their mindset and fast otherwise things were going to start going downhill quickly. I got them to look after Ryan at the weekends and in the school holiday while the nursery was closed to take their mind off the situation as much as I could.

My Sister and Brother in law were in disgust how I could let an ill man look after my child when I should be doing it myself. I explained that Ryan and Dad were best friends and It gave him something to get up for in the morning. It made Mum stop feeling sorry for herself and concentrate on her grandson. But they still didn't get it and I was called selfish. But I didn't care I knew what I was doing it for and that's all that matters. How things were going if I hadn't of stepped in he wouldn't have lasted another month.

Dad took me aside and asked for my help.

"I need you to deal with everything and soon, start getting everything together," he told me.

He could feel himself getting worse by the day and even though he had all the treatments he told me he got the results back and they hadn't worked, however, he wasn't ready to tell Mum and told me not to say anything either. I was stuck, do I abide by my Dad's wishes and say nothing and leave Mum to cope or do I tell her, so she gets used to the idea that he was going soon? I had a hard decision to make.

I left it a couple of days and I could see Dad was getting worse. She had to be told, but it was his place to tell her.

Work was going well but I could see Dad starting to struggle with getting up, walking and having energy to last the day. He was so worried about Mum's future. We sat and talked about all the financials and got everything sorted out.

I bought their Caravan, so the mortgage was paid, and everything was up to date, it was a struggle but I knew it had to be done for his peace of mind. I started seeing a new man from work. He knew everything about what I was going through with my parents and he got on well with Ryan, we had been friends for a couple of months and we decided to take it further. He had been the shoulder I needed with everything that was happening.

I explained to him that Dad was getting worse and I would have to give up work to look after them all. He would hear nothing of it.

"You're not giving up work, as I stay at yours often, I will give up work to look after Ryan, so you can work, you need to work to keep this place, so you can pay for Ryan and nursery, not only that, you won't have to pay out so much for nursery."

Because Dad was getting so bad, I'd upped Ryan's nursery to five days a week for twelve hours a day I was paying eight hundred a month in fees so, my parents were only having him on a Saturday. It would be nice to cut that to over half at least as I was struggling, so, I agreed.

Within a few weeks every day I was feeling guilty, I still hadn't sorted out my head from my son's Dad leaving us and I still had all his stuff around the house.

However, that was all on hold, so I could deal with the situation now, I had Ryan to sort out, Mum to keep calm and Dad to make sure he got to any appointments he needed to. I wanted to help him every way I could, I was also working full time and when I got in, I was shattered, I would go straight to bed, it wasn't a life right now it was all about survival in all aspects of my life, job, my child and my parents.

This wasn't fair, but I knew I had to let my partner go, I knew it was going to hurt him, but I had to do it. I had to think of how my actions were affecting him and I took him home to his parents and didn't return.

My dad passed away in hospital 16th March 2005 with his closest family beside him. That was one of the hardest days of my life. My hero, the strongest man I knew, my Daddy; was gone.

Dad took a turn for the worse so we called an ambulance to take him to the hospital, he was in so much pain but he was trying not to show it but I could see it in his eyes. They put him on the ward and gave him some pain killers. I sat next to him while he was sitting up in the bed drinking his cup of tea, smiling and joking with us.

Each of us took turns to have one to one time with him. I walked up to him and gave him a flash of a smile, he gave me a cuddle and told me he was sorry for how he acted in my childhood. He'd found it so hard to bring up a girl and could only treat me like a boy because that's all he knew. He didn't expect me to be as strong as I was. He told me he had wished that so many things could have been different between us. That he forgave me for how I reacted to the situations with bringing the police to the house and understood I was scared and that he was sorry that he put me in that situation in the first place.

That moment right there I looked into his eyes and they were filled with regret.

"I am so proud of the woman you have become, you turned out just perfect in the end. You have grown up into a beautiful strong woman with a beautiful son who I think the world of, never change who you are. You just need to find a decent man to accept the both of you, make it a good man. You're a strong and independent young lady who has everything going for you. You can be anything you want to be, never give up on what you want to achieve no matter how far you think you must go to get it. Be proud of yourself of who you have become, we all go through bad times in our life, but life is what we make of it, you have a big heart don't keep finding men that are bad for you. You have your head screwed on straight now go and find your happiness I will always be with you."

I gave him a big cuddle and told him I loved him. This was our last one to one conversation alone. Dad was in more pain and the pain killers were just not working anymore.

So, at 3pm they gave him his own room, to do this we knew the time was near, but he was still sitting up in bed smiling and drinking his tea. We told all the family to come and see him as we didn't know how much time he had to say their goodbyes.

At 4pm they gave him a morphine drip in his leg to numb the pain, he laid back on the bed and fell asleep. To keep his lips and mouth wet I was told by the nurse to swab his mouth every 15 to 20 mins so it didn't dry out.

He felt cold to touch so we covered him up to keep him warm. When we looked down, we noticed his feet and legs were swelling. We told the nurse that the drip was leaking out his leg. They moved his drip up to his tummy area. I asked the nurse why this was happening, she told me that with cancer patients they die from the feet up and the first sign was the swelling she told us it's only a matter of hours, as soon as it goes up to his organs and to his brain he would pass away.

Within a couple of hours the same had happened to his tummy so they stuck the drip into his neck. He was put on his side to face Mum and we left her, so she could talk to him.

By 10.45pm his breathing started to change, and she called us back in. I sat on the bed beside him and I gave him a cuddle and put my hand on his heart and just felt it slowly beating onto my fingers knowing it was going to be the last time I felt it. His heart slowed down, and I told mum it was time. Dad opened his eyes looked straight at Mum enough to say he was sorry for leaving her and took his last breath and his heart stopped tapping on my fingers.

Within 18 months my Hero was dead.

My mum fell to pieces, Dad had done everything for her for so many years it was going to be a struggle to adjust to not having him around. I'd promised Dad that I would be there for Mum no matter what.

It wasn't my time to grieve, my family needed me. I had to be strong and get things done. I was a twenty-six-year-old woman who had no choice but to hold it all together.

At the funeral my sister-in-law come up to me and said "You must be a hard cow, you're the only person in that room that didn't cry for your Dad".

What she didn't understand was that day wasn't for me, it was for my Mum and it was not my turn to grieve when I knew she could barely cope. I knew she needed me there and I knew I needed to be strong.

My ex-partner who looked after Ryan for those few weeks while I was at work told me he had made a promise to my dad that he would always be there for me and Ryan no matter what. To this day he has never broken that promise and has become one of my best friends.

MAXINE'S THOUGHTS AND TIPS

I have moments of grief right up to this day thirteen years later. I miss our chats, his dry sense of humour, his arms around me, his advice and even while writing this I have tears rolling down my face because it takes me back to that time of pain and how I felt in that moment. But I carry my promise with me every day I made to him. I will always push to keep moving forward in my life. In work and business, I don't always make the right decisions and I learn by my mistakes.

As you will find out in the next chapters of my life when I was left for dead.

My mum still grieves daily for the man she loves, and she is stuck at that hospital like Groundhog Day. If she lets go and accepts he has gone, then she has no choice but to move on and that is just something she's not ready to accept yet. She never went to see a bereavement counsellor after Dad and still hasn't to this day.

She doesn't want to move on because she is scared that if she does then she is letting him down by carrying on her life without him.

There is only so much you can do to help someone. You can only help them if they want to be helped. You never know when a trigger will happen you just need to be there when it does. I know she feels as though it should have been her with everything she has gone through herself. However, its life and it was just his time, and nothing can change that.

Be patient with a person who is grieving don't take their choice away when you feel they should stop. They will stop then they feel it's time too.

CHAPTER 9
REGRETS

I left my double-glazing job after Dad passed away. I needed time to spend with Mum to help her as much as I could. We got all the paperwork sorted together as Dad had already gone through everything with me.

Ryan and I needed some bonding time together. He was missing his Grandad and best friend. I needed to get to know him more and vice versa. I took him to the caravan where there were so many memories.

Memories of my Brothers, my Nan, my parents and myself as a child growing up. This place was like a second home to me. I took him to the beach to paddle in the water and throw stones out to sea, playing football on the field, mini bowling in the arcade and walking back and forth to the playground.

We had many hours of special bonding time and I was loving it but I still carried this big hole in my heart.

At the arcade there was this one guy that would always give Ryan his change and make conversation with him at every opportunity it was so nice to see him talking to someone and smiling. Every arcade we went into Ryan would always go back to the same guy to talk to him. Ryan called him change man. Change man and myself would stand and chat while Ryan was playing on the arcade machines and bowling.

After a few weeks I invited him around the caravan. He would come around on his lunch break, before and after work and we became close. Within two months we began seeing each other. It was great to see a smile on Ryan's face again and I was happier too. The three of us would go out to the Zoo and the beach; it was exactly what we both needed after losing Dad.

Within a couple of weeks there was a complication. He had only split with his girlfriend a few months before, she had moved out and he was living in her place. She found out we were seeing each other and gave him a choice. Leave me or leave the house and his dog. He chose, and she gave him a week to leave. I was only using the caravan at weekends and I had nobody renting it for a couple of weeks, so, I told him he could stay there while he was looking for another place to stay.

Two weeks later he still hadn't found anywhere to live, he didn't have enough money saved up to rent anywhere either for a deposit. I felt stuck between a rock and a hard place. I wasn't ready to have someone move in with me, but I also couldn't see him living on the streets either as I felt partly responsible for him not having a place to stay.

Knowing that he was leaving all his friends, his unfriendly dog, family and his work behind to start a whole new life with someone he had only known for three months. He wasn't ready either but also felt like he had no choice as his friends and family wouldn't let him stay with them either.

The first couple of weeks were a strain on the both of us. We had gone from seeing each other at weekends for a few hours a day to living with each other, but we had to try and make it work. I also noticed he had a very bad cannabis habit which cost him a thousand pound a month but with no income coming in and being seventy miles away from his dealer he was going cold turkey. I had now got myself in a situation that I was stuck with. I also found out that his family were paying all his bills, so his money could go on drugs. I was very confused about the whole situation, why would his parents happily pay his bills, so he could do that? I just didn't understand at all, but he never wanted to talk about it. He wouldn't let me close enough into his life to understand. I had to just deal with the situation and try and sort it out as we went along.

We made an agreement that he would get a full-time job and come off the drugs but do it slowly. I didn't want my child growing up thinking it was ok and I had accepted it, because I hadn't.

It was hard work but over the next few months he had got himself a job and got his habit down to two hundred pounds a month, he was happier in himself and things were getting better.

Everything seemed to be moving forward there was light at the end of the tunnel. As time went on, we were really bonding as a family. After everything that I had gone through with Ryan's Father I wanted to move from our house for a new start and to be closer to Mum, I'd got a second job to bring in extra income ready for the move.

Six months had gone by and things were going well. I carried on working my two part time jobs and every evening I would take him to work as he didn't drive and was on permanent night work.

It was Valentine's day, and in not such a romantic way he got down on one knee in a shopping centre car park while I'm sitting in the car dropping him off to work and he asked me to marry him. I said yes.

Without even putting the ring on my finger he handed me the box, closed the door and went to work. Not how I had imagined it would be, it didn't feel special, but I wasn't going to complain. I couldn't expect something extra if that person doesn't have a romantic personality, so I swept it aside and said nothing.

March 2006, we moved to our new house closer to mum. To make it cost effective and the fact he didn't like parties we had our engagement party and moving in party at the same time at our new house. That evening he walked up to me and said

"I want us to have five children and we should start straight away".

We hadn't spoken about children before it just never come up. I loved our family as it was, and I was happy, and I told him I didn't want any more children especially after the experience I'd had giving birth to Ryan.

After the party he was a completely different person.

He didn't speak to me for five days. When I did finally push to get a conversation to get it out of him what was wrong, we had the biggest argument. He was yelling at me about how selfish I was and that he would leave if I didn't change my mind about wanting more kids. I was stunned at his reaction. I'd never seen him like this before; he was so angry.

Ryan's birth was horrific, I was cut, he had to be suctioned out as he got stuck and I didn't want to go through it again, but Ryan would come up to me saying he wanted a little brother or sister to play with. It's what they both wanted, what do I do?

After a few days with everything swirling around my head, thinking about my past when I was with my boyfriend who couldn't have children and I knew I wanted them, I knew how he was feeling.

Perhaps I was being selfish, we sat down together and discussed my concerns about the birth, money and becoming a single parent and that I understood how he felt because I had been put into the same situation. We decided that we would have 1 child together.

However, the deal would be he would stay at home with him/her, so he got to see the babies first steps, laugh and words. As he had never been through it before and as it was going to be his only child, we both said we didn't want him missing anything. I also told him that by having this child he had to come off the cannabis all together.

It was agreed, he was so looking forward to having his own baby to love from the start. He promised me Ryan would be included with everything. I was still apprehensive about going through it all again, what if I was left as a single mum again, what if anything went wrong.

A month later I went for a routine smear test and after a few days I got a phone call. Congratulations you are pregnant. What already? I couldn't believe it had happened this quickly we had only been trying since the week before, we got a hospital appointment and went for our first scan.

"I'm afraid we can't test and measure your baby today", said the sonographer.

"You are going to have to wait until you are twenty weeks pregnant."

What!

We didn't understand, and she explained that I was too far through my pregnancy and I would have to wait.

"Well how far gone am I", I asked her.

I hadn't had any signs to say I was even pregnant.

"You won't have long to wait", she said, "you are fifteen weeks and four days into your pregnancy and the baby is due in November. "

I was gob smacked, this means I was already pregnant before we got engaged and before we moved to our new home. Now I started to worry, I had been carrying furniture and boxes while moving, took Ryan to Legoland for his birthday and I went on all the roller-coasters, I had eaten peanuts, eggs and been out with the girls and had a night drinking.

I went to the doctors to be safe and had some tests. They found I had gestural diabetes which is common if someone had PSOS (polycystic ovary syndrome). Now I knew I was pregnant I started showing that I was. Within weeks I had grown to a size twenty-four in clothes and I could balance my dinner plate on my belly and when I sat down my belly would be nearly to my knees. Luckily, I could sit down at work when I needed to. But as the weeks passed, I grew larger and I got sciatica down my right leg.

The pain was excruciating at times, it went from my bum cheek, into my groin and down my leg to my knee. I just couldn't get comfortable no matter how I sat or laid. My back was playing me up too because 18 months before I had taken Ryan to the park and on the roundabout, I fell off it backwards onto my coccyx bone. I had to crawl to my sister's house as I couldn't walk. A normal five-minute walk took me 2 hours to crawl.

I took many high dose painkillers, but I never did go to the doctor to get it checked out. Stupid of me really but like most of us do, we just get on with things. But with all this pain searing through my body I went to the doctor, there was nothing they could do until baby moved off one of my nerves that was causing me the sciatic pain. I couldn't wait to get this baby out.

At our twenty weeks scan I found out I was pregnant with a little girl (Jasmin) the time was getting closer and the three of us were looking forward to our new addition to the family.

In August we were discussing last names, this awful dread came over me. Did I suck it up and put the baby in his name? or did I put the baby in my name with Ryan's? I told him how I felt and what had happened in the past. That night we booked the wedding. We tried booking it for October before she was born however there wasn't enough time, money was an issue, no dresses would fit me at the size I was I was in too much pain to do anything.

So, we booked it for Saturday 13th January 2007.

Jasmin was due on the 9th November, but she was nowhere to be seen, I tried everything from hot curry to walking miles, to hot baths, nothing.

Until Sunday 19th November my contractions started at 9am. I had to call my friend as I couldn't drive, and neither could he.

By the time my friend got to me at 11am my contractions were five minutes apart, and within a half hour of us getting to the hospital they were 2 minutes apart.

We got to the ward and they rushed me in. It was Sunday and they only had skeleton staff. I was put on a monitor and left for a few hours, my contractions were getting stronger, but something was wrong, her heart beat kept going down to 20 where before it was on 50-60. I called the nurse concerned.

She told me that if her heart beat didn't pick up then I would have to go for an emergency C-Section. I was put into the labour room, but the heart beat wasn't going back up.

Another nurse joined the team and I told the nurse about my concerns, but it was falling on deaf ears. I kept calling her back in as I was worried, so she burst my waters as they hadn't gone on their own. There was so much fluid that the nurse had to come in with a mop and bucket. I'd already gone through the ten towels that's provided for a birth and it was still all coming out.

The pain was becoming unbearable and I got into an argument with the nurse over painkillers. She was telling me what I should be having next and when. That didn't sit right with me, I knew what I wanted and needed. I had been 5cm dilated for over an hour now, nothing was moving and the heartbeat was still dropping. I asked to see the doctor, I was told he is in surgery and I would have to wait until he was done as he was the only surgeon in the hospital as it was Sunday.

I saw the doctor and told him what had happened about the heartbeat, about the argument with the nurse about the painkillers and the emergency C-section. He checked me over and told me I should have gone down to have the baby out as she was too big for me, she was stuck, and the heart beat was getting lower. He told me the baby was in the birth canal and was now too late to do a C-section and I was just going to have to deliver the baby. I was so angry at the nurse for ignoring me. He gave me an epidural for my body to relax, I was a high-risk pregnancy anyway because of me having gestural diabetes but the doctor didn't know this either, otherwise I would have gone straight down to theatre.

The doctor stayed with me as it was too risky for him to leave. I got to ten centimeters dilated and now it was time to push.I felt like my insides were being turned inside out, I had searing pain running through my body where she was so big that she was stuck and taking my skin with her. She wasn't coming out, she was stuck, as soon as I pushed on a contraction when the contraction stopped, she went back up again. I could see the worried look on his face, "we need this baby out and now" he said. He used a suction cup as

143

soon as he saw the head, it didn't work, so he got his forceps, they didn't work either. He had one last choice to get this baby out, "I'm sorry", he sprayed this cold stuff on me and cut me from front to back, inside and out to make more space and he put both his hands inside me got hold of her head and dragged her out of me with a few forceful pulls.

There's no crying…….. they rushed her over and cleared her airways and gave her oxygen, she wasn't breathing. She was blue! My partner was just sitting there eating a jacket potato. They worked on her for over a minute, that was the longest minute of my life.

Jasmin came into this world on 19th November 2006 at 5.35pm the cord had been wrapped around her neck twice and every time I was having a contraction it was strangling her. When I finally saw her, she was blue with bright red lips and looked very peaceful after her ordeal.

I was absolutely shattered but seeing Ryan's beaming face that he had a new little sister was priceless. Ryan gave Jasmin her first bottle and she drank 4oz straight away and then two hours later another bottle of 8oz. She had been waiting for food as I hadn't eaten since the day before. Her colour had come back in her face. She was beautiful 8lb 2oz little girl.

She was kept in ICU for three days, so they could keep a close eye on her. However, we stayed in hospital for seven days in total, and by the end of it I was eager to get out and go home, so as we could have our family all together at last. When we got home I showed him the ropes from the start on what to do with Jasmin, nappy changes, bottle feeds, sleeping positions, how to make bottles etc.

MAXINE'S THOUGHTS AND TIPS

You know your body more than anyone else, if you think something isn't right then get a second opinion. If I hadn't of kept on at the nurses and rushed the Doctor down to me my daughter wouldn't be here today.

With the wedding fast approaching and Christmas coming we had to get some money in. I wasn't ready to go back to work, I still had all my stitches in and I had only been home from hospital four days, but I had no choice. I got in my car and slowly drove myself to work.

It was light duty as I was gift wrapping people's Christmas presents. It was only a temporary job, so I had to make the most of it. I went back on the 1st December as it finished on New Year's Eve. I had to push myself forward. I had no maternity pay and he was working nights but his money didn't cover much at minimum wage in a warehouse 3 days a week.

Within four weeks, things had changed, I just put it down to him being tired with the baby, so in the new year I stayed at home for a bit to spend time with the family. But I could see he was agitated, he would keep having a go at Ryan and pushing him out the way rather than including him.

It was only a week until the wedding and I was having worries whether he even wanted to go through with it. All he kept saying to me was he wanted nothing to do with the wedding he only wanted to turn up.

Alarm bells were ringing but I just put it down to being a new parent and the extra responsibilities.

Saturday 13th January 2007 the day was here for me to get married, I was fed up and I'd been crying before I'd even got out of bed. We had an argument the night before about the reception. The hall was booked out the night before and wouldn't let us in to decorate so my friends were doing it on the day after the ceremony. We had no money for a caterer, so I was doing the food myself with some help from mum and family.

My wedding dress was off the peg and it was more like an evening gown that didn't sit right, didn't flatter me and I hated it. I'd asked my sister to come dress shopping with me, but she was busy, Mum couldn't face wedding dress shopping. But I only had three weeks before my wedding to get one and nothing was fitting me yet due to having the baby, so my friend came with me.

The wedding was at 11am as the photographer said it would be too dark for photos any later. All 50 guests would have to cram in mums house as the hall was being decorated for the evening, I had to miss twenty of my family out because the place wasn't big enough which I was gutted about, and my dad wasn't walking me down the aisle.

All that was going through my head before I'd even got up. The wedding was on a shoestring and the only thing I liked was the wedding car. What else could go wrong...Famous last words!

On the way to Langton's registry office the car looked nice, but it was January it was draughty and had no heating and the driver had no blankets by the time I got there I was nearly blue. There was a mix up with the registrar signing, the outside photos everyone was freezing cold and wind swept.

We got back to Mum's and everyone had to stand side by side squashed in as there was no space to sit anywhere for the next three hours until the hall was ready. Mum's friend who was meant to going around to Mums before we got back to put the hot food on, was nowhere to be seen. So, in my so-called wedding dress I was cooking chili, bolognaise and jacket potatoes to warm everyone up.

My new husband who was meant to be talking to our guests had disappeared, I found him asleep upstairs. I could have cried the way everything had gone but instead I hit the roof and tried getting him out of bed, but he just stayed there.

When it was finally time to leave for the evening reception my new husband told me to go ahead of him, he will meet me there in a bit. I went back and checked on him ten minutes later and he had gone back to sleep. I knew getting married to him wasn't right and he was proving me right more and more. I felt I couldn't let people down and I couldn't be a single parent again, so I just went through with everything. His mum came up to me and said that I shouldn't have cut his drugs out.

She told me the reason why we made sure he was on them, was because they chilled him out. It was good for him to be chilled because he used to be a violent alcoholic and went for his mum with a baseball bat.

"And I'm getting told this now" I said to her.

My husband and I walked into the reception before anyone else to have a couple of pictures taken with the cake. He had the hump with me because he didn't like parties and didn't want to be there. People started to turn up, but the night went from bad to worse. We did the first dance that he didn't want to do. I got upset that I couldn't have a father and daughter dance. My brother tried to do a speech and we all broke down in tears about my Dad.

Eighty-two people didn't turn up for the evening receptions. Five black sacks of food got binned that we cooked and for most of the evening we spent the night apart from each other. At the end of the evening we were going to a hotel for the night that we had booked. My friend was having the kids for the night and the next day. However, when we told people we had to go in ten minutes because our taxi was getting there for midnight everyone left and it was just the two of us clearing the hall up. The taxi turned up and had to wait until we were finished. We got to the hotel and crashed out.

Next day we spent looking around the sites of London as we didn't want to go far because of the kids. By lunch time I phoned home and Jasmin had been crying all night and all day, but I was told not to go home.

"Enjoy your day", she said.

The problem was all I could think about was everyone at home.

The next couple of weeks were ok, however I couldn't get out of my head what his mum had told me. I thought back to when he moved in with me, now I understand why he couldn't go and live with his parents and why his Nan didn't accept him back into her flat. It also made sense now why they paid for all his bills, so he could go and get the drugs he needed, anything for a quiet nonviolent life.

Everything happened all in the space of 18 months we met, he moved in, we got engaged, moved to a new house, had a baby and got married. It made me more alert to any behaviour that I would see that was out of the ordinary.

February 2007 came, and I'd been off work now for nearly six weeks, money was running short so back to work I went, but what was I going to do now? I needed something I knew how to do but not to go backwards. I saw an advertisement to become an agency cook. It was perfect, I had been cooking for myself since I was ten and I could do the hours to suit me. Which was great for working around the kids.

My husband said he was happy to stay at home with the kids while I worked, which helped due to him still not driving, or having much experience with anything apart from arcade machines, kids rides and warehouse work and there wasn't much of that in walking distance. It started out three days a week for four hours a day working in the fire stations, then once people got to know how I worked I was getting bookings everyday if I wanted them.

I would come home from work and cook dinner and spend time with the kids and he would be on his PS3 all evening. Not wanting to talk or interact with me in any way.

Every week I was coming home and finding he had bought another £50 game to play on. I pulled him up on it when I looked at our joint bank account and the rent, council tax and direct debits were bouncing. All the money I was earning he was spending it the day it came in and putting us into debt. He was giving me snide comments that I was doing what I was good for and working, that I should start working seven days a week, so the bills could be paid. He would say to me that the only reason why he married me was that he had nothing better to do that day and has regretted it ever since. He would sometimes be quite paranoid that I was out working all the time while he was stuck in the house with the kids. But any spare time I spent with him, why would he think that? I think it's time you went back to work I said to him sitting at home constantly is doing nobody any good. I paid for him to have his CBT test and we went and got him a scooter.

Warehouse work was the only thing that he had experience with since he had been with me and not many companies wanted to take him on. He finally got a job working nights taking in deliveries.

Before long I was cooking at work seven days a week, however, in the evenings I was just sitting there doing nothing as he was at work, twiddling my thumbs. I took up another job working behind the bar at a pub 3 evenings a week (Thursday, Friday and Saturday), just to give myself something to do as I was just sitting in the house, the kids asleep, I might as well make the most of my time and bring some more money in that he was spending.

Things were going from bad to worse, every evening before I got home he had put the kids to bed so I didn't get chance to see them, every time Jasmin woke up he went and sorted it out and he wouldn't let me go in there.

"I don't know why you are even here, you might as well go to work, nobody wants you here anyway, you're just getting in the way" I was gob smacked and devastated all at the same time. I turned and shouted at him

"I worked hard because I would bring more money in, I worked hard so he could see your daughters first everything, I worked even harder because you are spending the money like water and when I do get a chance to be part of the family you have put the kids to bed and you're ignoring me all evening"

I got nothing back. He didn't even look at me. I might as well have saved my breath.

With all the hours I was working in the kitchen my sciatica was playing me up. I couldn't keep doing all these hours on my feet. I had to change jobs. I went to the doctor and he told me my body was too heavy for my legs and I had to lose weight, if I didn't, then within the next three years I would be on crutches, I was desperate to get something done as my BMI was just over 40 and I was nearly seventeen stone. He put me on the gastric band waiting list, however that was five years long. I couldn't wait but I had no choice.

I started working at a timeshare company as one of the managers, I was still cooking part time, but it got me off my feet and into an office.

Exceeding all my targets from the time I started the job another lady who worked beside me who had been there for ten years took a complete dislike to me and on a few occasions tried to get me fired. I wasn't just exceeding my targets but also getting a better result than her every month and I was making her look bad. I didn't stay very long as office politics isn't my thing. However, before I left there was this couple that came into my office.

She was a doctor and he was a gastric surgeon.

Perfect I thought, we got talking and we exchanged numbers to see what he could do to help me. I went to Maidstone and we discussed everything about the sciatica in my pregnancy, me falling off the roundabout and what the doctor had said about the crutches, but when it came down to money I just didn't have £5,500 to pay for it.

We made an agreement, I would have the surgery in the next few months I would pay him a deposit and that every time I went for a "band fill" I would pay him money to whatever I could afford at the time. Every couple of months I went back and paid him a few hundred pounds at a time.

MAXINE'S THOUGHTS AND TIPS

Having a gastric band was one of the best things I've ever done, however it takes a lot of commitment. Within 18 months I had gone from nearly 17 stone down to 9 stone. But, that's with me going back and forth to the hospital getting a gastric fill to make the band tighter every two months, I had clothes that fitted me and I felt great, I also didn't have any pains either.

There was negatives to me having it done too. Because I lost weight so quickly I got Gallstones and I was hospitalized for four days, and for two years I was mainly eating liquid food. £5,500 is a lot of money to give over so make sure you have money behind you, I was lucky that the surgeon helped me. And even though I looked fantastic in my clothes I had a lot of excess skin that I couldn't afford to get removed after. Make sure you consider all the options before you go under the knife.

Jasmin was now 2 and a half, nothing had gotten any better between us. I just sat in the car and stared at the house. How did I get here? I said to myself, my life wasn't a bed of roses, every time we see each other we didn't talk, I didn't get to spend much time with the kids. I was now working 3 jobs one in a film production company, cooking in the evening and working behind the bar at the weekend.

I just carried on sitting in the car staring, I wonder how things are going to be today. Not wanting to go in the house straight away I cleared my car out of rubbish. I walked to the dustbin to put the rubbish in there and I see four empty beer cans. Every emotion was running through my head. How long had he been drinking for? How many did he really have today? Then the thoughts came through about what his mum had said to me on our wedding day.

But I got in and said nothing, and that night was the same thing, he just sat on the PlayStation. So, I got in said hello and sat at the computer. Needing conversation, I began chatting to a few of my girl-friends online to pass the time until bedtime. The computer was in the living room next to the TV. I tried to make conversation, but still I got nothing from him except a grunt.

I went out into the kitchen to fetch a juice and he followed me. He asked if I was cheating on him, "No I'm not cheating on you and never would, I don't get time to cheat" He called me a liar and punched me in the face. In shock I stepped back. I couldn't believe what he had just done. I shouted at him that he was insane. He punched me again and put me in a headlock, put me onto my knees and punched me in the mouth, head and eyes.

With every punch my head hit the kitchen concrete floor, the pain in my head was unbearable and all I could do was count as he was repeatedly punching me. I felt this massive pain in my mouth as I was spitting blood. He had punched me in my mouth so hard that my tooth came clean out from the root. My son Ryan who was six-year-old ran into the kitchen after hearing my screams of pain and shouted at him

"DADDY PLEASE STOP HURTING MY MUM".

He stopped and let go of me out of my headlock and I laid on the floor in a heap crying with Ryan cuddling me. My son saved my life that day.

But the night wasn't over. He had gone into the living room, and was sitting there sobbing saying, "Oh my God, what have I done".

I walked into the living room. "I'm so, so sorry I don't know what came over me to do that. I've mucked everything up, I've lost everything now. I'm so stupid", he said through his tears. I sat next to him, I know you have been drinking I told him. How long has it been going on I asked him? "A couple of weeks" he said. I was so angry that I had been working my backside off trying to support this family working extra hours to make up the money he is spending on games and now he has been drinking while looking after both our children. I was livid. However, I had just got a beating, I didn't want another so I kept my mouth shut.

My face was burning, my head was hurting so much, my jaw was throbbing, and my eyes were swelling. I told him I needed to go to the A&E to get checked over. I felt so angry as he knew what I had gone through with my Dad, all I could think of was "how dare you". I told him he had to come with me and face the music for what he had done. I got the kids a sitter and I drove the car there with him in the passenger seat.

I got to the A&E and the receptionist saw the mess of my face and I was seen within 10 minutes. I got my husband to come in with me, the doctor sat me down and asked the question this is bad who did this to you? And I pointed at my husband.

The doctor was shocked that he was there, and he was about to call the Police and Social Services when they found out we had children. I told him not to! I bought him with me, so he could sit there and watch the pain I now must go through to get this sorted.

"It is the first and only time that he will do this to me, it will never happen again. He is going to get some counselling and stop drinking."

The doctor ordered a head scan as he thought I had a fractured skull and a possible fractured jaw. After a few X-Rays and hours in A&E he hadn't fractured my skull, or broke my jaw, however, I definitely had concussion and was told not to sleep the rest of the night.

We got home he said he was sorry and made a lot of promises.

No more drinking, No more lashing out and that he would get counselling to get to the core of his addiction problems.

The next day I got an appointment with the dentist. I had a huge gaping hole where my tooth was, and it was sore. The dentist told me that I had broken the part of my jaw where the tooth sits in. He was taking fragments of bone out my mouth where it was poking out my gum. I needed to get the gap covered as quick as possible. A bridge was ordered to cover the gap at the front of my mouth.

MAXINE'S THOUGHTS AND TIPS

My biggest regret is I didn't go to the police and at least report it. So at least it was on record. I just thought it was a one-off thing that would never happen again.

Nothing more was mentioned to Ryan about the incident, which in hindsight now I should have spoken to him about it, so he could get closure on what he saw. It's a regret that I will carry with me for the rest of my life because it's something that haunts him even to this day.

If a child you know has seen domestic violence and your worried about them these are the signs that you should be looking for, they may become: anxious or depressed, have difficulty sleeping, have nightmares or flashbacks, easily startled, complain of physical symptoms like tummy aches, wet their bed, temper tantrums and problems with school, behave much younger than they are, become aggressive or withdraw from other people, have a lowered sense of self-worth, begin to play truant, start to use alcohol or drugs, begin to self-harm by taking overdoses or cutting themselves or have an eating disorder.

Some children may also feel angry, guilty, insecure, alone, frightened, powerless or confused. They may have ambivalent feelings towards both the abuser and the non-abusing parent. However, you don't know what's going on behind closed doors, the best thing to do is call a domestic violence helpline to get some advice, just in case anything is aimed at the child and you go to a family member and make it worse for the child.

I carried on going to work and told people I had been mugged because it made it easier not to answer their questions or be judged by them for not throwing him out. But what they didn't understand at the time is my biggest fear wasn't my husband, it was becoming a single parent of two children age six and sixteen months. I had to weigh up the odds and my safety came last. I see now that was the completely wrong way to look at it. I should have kicked him to the curb right then, however, I learnt from the experience with my Dad and alcohol that everyone deserves a second chance and everyone makes mistakes.

I hid away from friends and family for three weeks until all the bruising and swelling had gone down. He started his counselling and things were working out great. It was my school reunion coming up that I had organized, and I was going to see many of my friends from school that I hadn't seen in fifteen years, it was about time I got out the house and had a bit of fun. However, my husband made it quite clear he wanted to come with me.

At the school reunion there were so many people to catch up with and it was nice to let my hair down and have some fun. My husband was back and forth to the bar all evening with pints of Coke, so I thought, I took a mouthful and found it was vodka. I was furious, but I didn't want to make a scene, next minute he came back from the bar drinking a WKD. I just stared at him. I didn't want to make an argument in front of forty people I had known from school. So, we left early (excuse to get the kids). He was stroppy on the way home because we had left early; I just didn't talk to him. I got home and went to bed.

CHAPTER 10
BROKEN ABUSED LEFT FOR DEAD

After an argument he walked out the door, just another day in the house. I took the kids to the park, "Do you want to go and see nanny?" I asked them.

They loved going to see their nan because she spoiled them, and they got lots of cuddles, not only that she lived just across the road from the beach. Two birds one stone, I thought. She lives just over an hour away and we spent the afternoon with her.

About three hours into our visit my Husband walks through the door explaining to his Nan that he had gone to visit a "girlfriend" (they had fancied each other for years) and he thought he would stop by, not knowing I had just heard everything he just said. The shock on his face when he saw us was startling; all I got was a harsh response of "What you are doing here at MY nans house".

At home that night I questioned him, but he got all sneaky and angry about it every time I mentioned her. I knew what went on even though he hadn't told me.

I couldn't live like this anymore; my life was the worst it could get. At every opportunity he would tell me I'm not needed in this family, I'm useless at everything I do, him or the kids didn't love me, he regretted meeting me and wished I had never come back to see him, I had no life, I didn't see my children, we argued every time we saw each other. I wanted out of the relationship, but I feared what he might do. I wouldn't have put it past him to take Jasmin away, never to be seen again.

It never got out of my head what he did to me previously and I was worried that if I left and took the kids with me I would always be looking over my shoulder. I was stuck in this life, but I had to try and change things slowly. The first thing we did was move to a new house, drastic I know but we had to get rid of the bad energy that was there.

Afterwards I took a few months off work and stayed at home with the kids. After a few "good" days we sat down for a talk. We agreed that things need to change, he said to me he wanted to go to work full time. He found a well-paying job and worked Monday to Friday. It gave him some well-deserved freedom and I got to spend some quality time with the kids, as before I would only see them for about an hour a day. It was nice taking them to the park, cinema, to go and see my mum and spend time with her and catch up with friends that I had lost touch with over the last couple of years due to me working so much.

My husband was missing spending time with the kids as it was such a big change so once every couple of weeks it would be daddy and kids time and I would go out with the girls. He told me to go out and enjoy myself.

This arrangement we had was working out fantastic, the kids saw the both of us, I had got my family back, got to go out with my friends more and not just work and he got to go out to work, meet new people and come home and enjoy his time with the family. This great set up carried on for almost seven months. Until he put a spanner in the works and didn't see why he should go to work all day and why I should go out every other weekend with my friends, why should he have to pay all the bills with HIS money it was his to spend how he wanted!

It was non-stop arguments about how I had slogged my guts out the last few years for this family with him spending every bit of money we had on stupid computer games. He stood over me shouting at me, spitting in my face then threw a Dyson hoover at me, I moved quick enough that it smashed on the floor but with the force it ripped a two-inch hole in the carpet.

I shouted at him "I suppose you're going to moan now you have to put your hand in your pocket and buy a new hoover as you have just smashed this one to pieces". He went for me and I cowered in the corner shaking.

Me and my big mouth! But it was the first sign of me starting to rebel, I knew for a fact it was all downhill from now on. Enough was enough and once I'd got to this stage in a relationship there was no turning back for me. I started closing my feeling down, I told him that after everything we had been through and how he had made me feel scared for my life, it was over.

I felt relieved that I had said it, worried about the outcome but we couldn't carry on like this. It wasn't a good environment for the children to see us argue. Also, for me having the flashback from when he was drinking and beat me and I'm that scared in a corner shaking, that just wasn't me.

A few days later we had a heart to heart. I couldn't just throw him out the house as he had nowhere to go and I didn't want the kids see me treat him that way. So, we agreed that I would look for a place for him to live, I even said to him I would pay his first month's rent. We both agreed it would be for the best. I told him he could see the kids whenever he wanted.

But 2 months later he was still there, we were not really on talking terms. We both just got up did the things we needed to do, sort the kids out, go to work and there had been no arguments at all.

Come January 2011 it was our four-year anniversary and he asked me if I would like a trip away to Canterbury for the weekend and his parents had already agreed to have the kids for the weekend. This was the first time they had ever had them. I was a little confused why he would even ask me as we were no longer a couple.

"It's an anniversary treat we are still married that's the least I can do to make up for the last few months and as a thank you for not throwing me out the door when you should have done".

I thought why not see how it goes, however I made it very clear that it didn't mean we were back together.

The last time we were away together was a weekend in London for our honeymoon. So, off to Canterbury we went. We had an amazing weekend, it was full of laughter and fun. We went sightseeing, visiting old buildings and walking down the cobbled streets. This is what we had been missing since we had got back. We hadn't had time to ourselves in four years, we forgot about us and just had the kids constantly or working.

MAXINE'S THOUGHTS AND TIPS

This is one of married couples' biggest mistakes in life, they don't spend any time together as just the two of you. Life passes us by with work and children and we just carry on with the same routine day in and day out and the next thing you see is you both have no feelings for each other anymore, or you have nothing in common and you grow apart, or you just don't stop on life's roller coaster.

You need to be just be in that moment, just the two of you, cherishing the love you have between each other. For us it was a little bit too long before we realised this, and things had fallen apart too much already.

You see the problem is even though we were still living together all the things he had said to me in the past stuck with me. How much he didn't want me, that he only married me for something to do and that him and the children didn't want me at home really bought my self-esteem down, it was through the floor. I tried to get back up by going out with the girls to make myself feel better and he saw my confidence was building back up, so he had to bring me down again. By throwing the hoover at me and seeing the fear in my eyes he knew he had put in my place.

He also knew that after I had made the decision, we were over there was no going back, that I'd stopped caring and loving him because there were no arguments and no conversations between us. He was leaving me to it, so I would forgive him before he showed me he still loved me, by putting the effort in and taking me away for the weekend.

The thing is when your partner is like this it shows more about them than it does about you. He was insecure, lonely and deep down really needed me. He had no friends, felt trapped and didn't go out anywhere. On one hand he would tell me to go out and then in the other he would get the hump that I had gone out and left him. I felt like no matter what I did I could never win, it was always wrong.

There are a lot of things I would do differently if that was now. I would have called off the wedding. Not worked so many hours, I regret not seeing my kids for a couple of years and my relationship with my daughter has suffered because I wasn't in her life much the first two years of it as I was always at work. Left the first time round and reported him to the police. However, I can't change past regrets, I can only learn by them and make sure I don't make the same mistakes in the future.

Talking about making mistakes.......
Here is what happened next.

Within twenty-four hours of us being back home he had changed from smiles and laughter to angry, miserable and moody. It felt like the whole weekend was a waste of time and money.

The next few weeks nothing had changed; he was still being moody and now secretive about something, something was going on, but I couldn't put my finger on it.

I carried on doing my thing and taking the kids out and having fun, he didn't want to join us, so I left him to it.
This particular weekend was all planned out. Visiting family all

day Saturday and out with friends to the beach with all the mums and kids on Sunday. The kids were looking forward to spending time with their friends too and going to the beach with their bucket and spades.

MAXINE'S THOUGHTS AND TIPS

This next part of my life is why I decided to write my book, there are going to be graphic details in the next section of my story, I wanted to tell you this first because its not for the faint hearted but I hope it gives you true hope in your heart that if I can get past this adversity in my life you can overcome anything in your life. This part of my story I told on stage at the Yes You Can Inspire to Achieve in August 2018 and I became an award-winning public speaker out of twenty-eight people.

I now want to tell my story to the world to help anyone who has gone through or going through the same situations in their life or of someone that they know like I have. I'm going to take you on a journey and I would like you to join me... This is my award-winning speech.

Everyone has a day when everything in your life changes. That one day were your life will never be the same again. This day happened to me. This day for me was Sunday 13th March 2011. I want you to join me on my journey.

My day started like any normal day I just didn't expect that day to end the way it did. I had booked a day off work and I was taking the kids down the beach with some girlfriends and their children. Lots of talking, laughing and eating ice cream. It was a great day.

Later in the afternoon my husband had been texting and calling me for the last 2 hours and he seemed agitated. Wanting to know when I would be home and how long I was going to be. We drove home at about 6pm and the kids and I were happily singing in the car on our 45 min journey.

"We're home I told them".

Out the car we got my eight-year-old son on one hand and my four-year-old daughter in the other hand. It had been such a great day. I didn't get many days off when working three jobs and just getting through paying the bills every month. I opened the front door and smelt cigarette smoke. I was confused. My brain was like,

"What the heck is going on here he only smokes outside and never in the house"

I got quite agitated. I open the door to the living room and there was my husband passed out on the sofa, thirty beer cans all over the floor, sofa and table. A dozen cigarette ends stamped out in the carpet, the whole living room was a total mess and smelt like a dirty pub. I get a flash back – my husband was a recovering alcoholic and been off the drink 2 years before I met him. But 18 months previously he fell off the wagon. Knocked the living daylights out of me.

Seven punches to the face while hitting my head against the concrete floor and knocking my tooth clean out my mouth breaking my jaw into fragments where my tooth should have been. My 6-year-old son saved my life by shouting at him. Snapping him out of it.

I went to the hospital for them to check me over. I took Dave with me to make him feel terrible for what he had done to me, I made sure he had to go through everything with me. I had a brain scan, and a head X ray. I left the hospital with two black eyes, two fat lips, a concussion and a missing tooth. I was lucky the doctor told me.

Dave sat there and cried. He was sorry.

Everyone deserves a second chance, right? So, back to Sunday 13th March, I walked in to the living room. Why didn't I just leave I hear you ask…. I panicked! I could hear my heart thumping in my chest. My brain was going at a hundred miles an hour. I told the kids to get upstairs and put their PJ's on. I sneaked upstairs behind them making sure not to wake him. I went into my bedroom and called my brother.

"Come quick, he's has had a lot to drink and I feel like something is going to go down, hurry"

As I put the phone down he was in the doorway.
"WHO ARE YOU ON THE PHONE TO?
He shouted at me.

"My brother, he's going to pop round for a bit"
"YOUR BROTHER ISN'T GOING TO SAVE YOU THIS TIME"
And WACK……. I fell onto the bed.

My face was pounding. I'm in a 12ft x 12ft room with a bed and wardrobes with my husband standing in the doorway. I had no way out. I climbed across the bed to get away from him, he got a hold of my hair from behind, dragged me off the bed and smashed my face up against the wardrobes. My face was hurting.

WACK! WACK!

Two more punches to the face. I go to run, but he punches me to the ground and stamps on my head as hard as he could and then on my legs continually.

"Max get up! I say to myself, get up and run!" BANG!

With all his might he puts me back down with one-foot smashing into the base of my spine. Ouch…. The pain…. I'm going to die…I'm scared for my life right now. I look into his eyes and all I can see is hate

"I need to leave right now".

He grabs my hair and drags me across the room continually punching me in the face. All I can feel is wetness coming out of my ears, my eyes, my mouth and my nose. I touch it, its blood.........I try and protect my face but it's just no use.i have nothing left to give, I can no longer feel the pain. I just feel his hand knocking against my skin. I look up and I see my 8-year-old son in the doorway with the look of TERROR on his face – I'm sorry son.

My four-year-old daughter comes marching in the bedroom and stands on the bed hands on her hips "don't touch my Mum" shouting at her dad at the top of her voice but he carries on punching me and kicking me in the face and just keeps coming.

Omg! She's too close, one punch from him and she's dead. She is going to get hurt. I've got to step up here. I'm her mum.

STOP!!!!
Please stop I scream with all my might.

STOP!!!! Please one more punch and our kids are going to see you murder their mum in front of them. Don't do this to the kids!

He stopped, "Where's the car keys?" down stairs, I said, and he left.

I lay there slumped up against the wall, the kids helped me into the bathroom "lock the door" I shouted and just listen.
There was silence...
The first thing Jasmin said to me was "Mummy are you going to die?"
"No Jasmin I'm not going to die. Ryan go downstairs and get the phone!"

I called the police and the ambulance. They both turned up with my brother in tow. I can see the guilty look on my brother's face. The police took my statement of events, and then the policewoman said,

"We need to know where he is so we can arrest him, can you call him?"

He had also taken my phone, so I couldn't call anyone. I've got to be strong, he is out there in my car driving after drinking over thirty cans, I don't need another set of parents going through losing a son or daughter like mine did due to reckless drink driving.

Give me the house phone I will call him "It's me, where are you? I know you didn't mean it, I love you, come back so we can sort this all-out" he put the phone down on me! He was on the A12.

The policewoman was confused. I explained that my parents had a caravan that every weekend of my life as a child I'd travelled that road and I know the sound of that road. He's on the A12.

My whole body was hurting; I needed to go to the hospital straight away. I told the doctor that he had stamped all over my body, they gave me a head scan and jaw scan. I had a concussion, I was bleeding from the ear, luckily my eardrum was still intact. I had no fractures to my head jaw or cheeks. He had punched and stood on my fingers and I couldn't move my little finger but again it wasn't broken. They were so surprised over the amount that he had hit me and kicked me. They told me that most people wouldn't have survived the blows and they were shocked how I didn't have any broken bones.

I asked for a full body scan as my back was hurting but they said no, I didn't need one. I felt something wasn't right but who am I to argue. I was sent home with strong painkillers. They found him the next day in the pub, the car was written off as he had hit a raised bank at 50mph and crushed the front end and the bottom of the car. The car flew around twelve metres in the air before hitting the ground. They arrested him, put him in the cell for 24 hours.

On his release he would constantly be ringing me, harassing me and being hateful, he was also ringing my place of work to be nasty down the phone. Three days later he was re-arrested for harassment. He was put back in the cell for 24 hours, whilst I got an injunction put in place, so he wouldn't come back to finish the job especially after I'd just had him arrested twice. The day of the court hearing I was told not to be there as there was no need and they found him guilty. Not of attempted murder. Not of GBH – as hospital reported no broken bones. Not of drink driving - as they couldn't prove he was drunk as they found him in the pub the next day. His sentence was for ABH - Aggravated vehicle taking & Harassment – Guilty!

I wasn't very happy that he had got away with the drink driving, however, off to prison he went for 8 months. He was out of our life and we could move on. I have been left with physical and emotional pain. That day not only did I have stamp marks all over my body and face I was left with a broken back.

The hospital refused the full body scan; however, they would have uncovered that he had shattered my L4 and L5 of my spine. I found this out months later when I finally had gotten an MRI done through my doctor as I was living off painkillers every day and I was still in pain with my back and I had to give up work to rest it.

They told me that the damage he had caused was like that of a car crash victim and I was very lucky not to be in a wheelchair. Now I have osteoarthritis of the L4 & L5 and an ear that pulsates and becomes very painful, I get ear ache every time I lay on it. I have a little finger that has taken six years to be able to use properly and, in the winter, gets very stiff and painful.

The kids have been left with the trauma and years of counselling. Ryan gets Panic Attacks, Anxiety when he hears people getting aggressive, he doesn't like shouting, he has gone through Depression and self-harmed by pulling his hair out, he keeps himself to himself and gets close to nobody.

Jasmin has aggressive behaviour, ADHD, Tourette's, panic attacks, anxiety disorder and attachment disorder. She is very outspoken has very low self-esteem, has self-harmed by biting herself and leaving bruising all over her arms and acts as though she will never be a victim. All these could have been bought on by the trauma.

And for all that the kids and myself have gone through he only got eight months and served four.

Standing at that door.
So why didn't I just leave?
I didn't feel like I had a choice.
My self-esteem was so low I just put up with everything.
It was the norm for me.

My dad was a drinker and would hit me after a night of drinking. Then once he was sober, he would say sorry give me a cuddle and give me money or go and buy me something.

Mum was in and out of hospital when I was younger.
She had cancer. She missed out on giving me lots of love, kisses and cuddles so her way of showing me love - she became a feeder.

I was bullied at school constantly from infant school right up to the last year of senior school "Big Mac and Roseanne Barr were my nicknames" you all remember her in the 90's right?

Just to make sure he didn't find us not only had I left my job because of my back, we moved to a new house in a new area and the kids moved schools just in case he came back for either one of us.

A long-time friend moved in with us to make sure we were not alone just in case he came back for us, one thing led to the other and we became an item. I felt safe with him around and I trusted him, we had known each other since college and always got on fantastically with him and the kids already knew him as he was there while they were growing up. It was a fresh start for all of us.

However, for fourteen months I could not work because of the pain in my back. I would lay on the sofa as much as I could taking painkillers just to get through every day. I was in constant pain, but I tried not showing it to anyone especially the kids. Instead of lying there feeling sorry for myself I wrote an 80-page business plan. Party Crown Direct! I'm going to run my own business I promised myself. He may of broke my back, but he didn't break my spirit.

MAXINE'S THOUGHTS AND TIPS

That was my award-winning speech I hope it helped you to understand what I had been through that night and everything that I have gone through in my life to get me where I am today.

After my adversity I got so much help from outside, don't ever think you are on your own because you are not. Victim Support, Women's Aid, Mind Councillor, Family Mosaic, Corium, Child Counsellors, Play Therapy. All these people stepped up to help me and my children. Don't be too proud to get the help, I did, and it was amazing. I will put some numbers at the end of the book for you.

A couple months after the incident I found out that my husband had Borderline Personality Disorder. If you feel you may have a loved one who might have this, I have listed the symptoms below to help you understand what that is.

Fear of abandonment - Terrified of being abandoned or left alone. A loved one getting home late from work or going away for the weekend can trigger intense fear. Frantic efforts to keep people close. Beg, cling, start fights, jealousy, track movements of a loved one, physically stop them person from leaving. Drives others away.

Unstable relationships - Relationships that are intense and short-lived, fall in love quickly, believing each new person is the one who will make you feel whole, only to be quickly disappointed. Relationships either seem perfect or horrible, nothing in between. Lovers, friends, or family feel like they have emotional whiplash from your rapid swings between idealization and devaluation, anger, and hate.

Unclear or unstable self-image - Sense of self is unstable. One-minute feel good about themselves, other times they hate themselves even view themselves as evil. No idea of who they are or what they want in life, frequently change jobs, friends, lovers, religion, values, goals, and even sexual identity.

Impulsive, self-destructive behaviours - Engage in harmful sensation-seeking behaviours when upset. Impulsively spend money, binge eat, drive recklessly, shoplift, engage in risky sex, or excessive drugs or alcohol. These risky behaviours make them feel better in the moment, but they hurt you and those around you over the long-term.

Self-harm - Suicidal behaviour and deliberate self-harm, thinking about suicide, making suicidal gestures or threats, or carrying out a suicide attempt. Self-harm includes all other attempts to hurt yourself without suicidal intent. Common forms of include cutting and burning.

Extreme emotional swings - Unstable emotions and moods, one moment feeling happy, and the next, despondent. Little things can put them into an emotional tailspin, mood swings are intense, but pass quickly, usually only lasting just a few minutes or hours.

Chronic feelings of emptiness - Feeling empty, a hole or a void inside them, feel you're "nothing" or "nobody." Feel uncomfortable, fill the void with drugs, food, or sex. But nothing feels satisfying.

Explosive anger - Intense anger, short temper, trouble controlling yourself with yelling, throwing things, or consumed by rage. spend a lot of time being angry at yourself.

Feeling suspicious or out of touch with reality - Struggle with paranoia, suspicious thoughts about others' motives. When under stress lose touch with reality, dissociation, may feel foggy, spaced out, or outside their own body

Abusers don't abuse every day they have many good days where they are loving and respectful, treat you to dinner and make you laugh. There are days when they say all the right words. But just because he/she is having a good day, they are still an abuser.

If you find yourself becoming an abuser:

Understand why your angry, you may be angry due to FEAR – if you feel threatened you are responding with a fight response. Ask yourself what you are afraid of? You may have lost a loved one and need some bereavement counselling.

It could have come from your past childhood where there was a lot of anger and you haven't gotten over your past and it's become your present and your future then have counselling sessions to help you leave the past in the past, you can't change what has happened, close that chapter and start a new one.

Mental wellbeing is all about having self-esteem and self-confidence without these we cannot feel contentment and enjoyment, engage with other people.

Connecting with others and having relationships are the first steps. Build up your self-confidence, have a sense of achievement, tell yourself you can do this and you will do whatever it takes to get there which will give you the confidence to try other new things.

Give to others – like I'm doing right now, by giving you my thoughts and feelings you know you are not alone and at some point, in our life most of us have been there. I give you my story to let you know that no matter how bad it gets. You are alive and that's a beautiful gift all on its own.

There is always a light at the end of the tunnel, that no matter how far away it is, all you must concentrate on is that next step. Before you know it, you'll be there.

So here I am. I am a survivor and I'm not suppressing my story any more, it's far too important! I want to help other people recognise they have a choice. Are you in a toxic relationship? Do you feel you're in a dead-end job? Are you in a situation where you feel stuck? Then CHANGE IT! Only you can do it. It's YOUR choice. Take it and don't let fear stop you because fear is your biggest enemy. Never let your past define your future. You are too important – if you believe in yourself then anything is possible. You have one life live it the way YOU want to live it and enjoy that journey.

This hindsight that I spoke about before just keeps coming back. The more I write this to you the more things I see how I went wrong in my life. The way I was, the way I acted, the way I let others get away with so much.

Every relationship I get into now my eyes are wide open. I don't get blinded by love, I don't get walked all over and I tell myself every day that I am worth it. That any man who wants to stand next to me must give me love, respect, honesty, faithfulness, loyalty and comfort and I shall give that back in return. I will not take anything less and until I find that one special person, I will stay single. I know my worth and I'm not afraid to say no to what I don't need. I'm not afraid to stand my ground in what I believe in and how I want to live my life. I am the most humble and grounded person who treats everyone with respect, but I expect the very best for myself because I'm worth it and I love myself with all my heart, so I know I'm ready to love another.

Being single – means you are strong enough to enjoy life without being with the wrong person. Life is a journey that will be full of experiences and learning curves enjoy them because this is the time you will grow. If we didn't have them our journey would be a very boring one. But maybe with a fewer grey hairs.

This is for you to know YOU have a choice in life. Life will throw you many curve balls but it's the way you react in those situations that count. Always have a positive mental attitude to every situation because everything you go through in life is a lesson. Learn from them and grow. Everyone has the courage of a lion it's just believing that you do.

I hope you enjoyed this book and it helps you on your journey and remember: You're Amazing!

Come back for Book 2 this is where you will find out what happened to me after my trauma of that dreadful day. And how it became one of the best days of my life.

Book number two will take you through How I came from being broken, abused and left for DEAD to how I raised myself up from the ashes to build my confidence and self-esteem. To become the FEAR FIGHTER, I am today.

Book number 2 will detail how I got over being told I was unemployable and that I will never work again. Also, when I was told I would possibly be in a wheelchair in two years' time to how I set my business up Party Crown Direct, because of my broken back, how I overcome FEAR and became an award-winning Public Speaker and having the confidence to tell you my story.

I will be going through how I overcome FEAR to become confident in front of the camera to become the Head of Broadcasting for Yes You Can Inspired to Achieve Global TV.

I will go through how I became a life and confidence coach through my obstacles and experiences I've been through.

How I came to write my own book, even though I'm dyslexic.

I will explain to you how I met my coaches and mentors Adam Stott and Bradley Chapman who have both helped me through my businesses in many ways. Getting me to think outside the box and stretch my mind.

2018 was a huge turn around for me in my life. I moved forward in more ways that I could have ever imagined, overcoming so many obstacles that I had kept with me.

Some for the last 30 years of my life, buried beneath the surface, but enough to keep me there and stuck.

But no more 2019 is looking even more amazing already. With work coming in from different sources. There is so much more to tell you.

Life is an amazing journey of self-discovery, learning lessons and experiences with many highs and lows.

With so many lows in my life I'm still here, writing this to you because it's NOT what you go through it's how you come out of it on the other side. And I can hold my head high saying, I DID IT!

I want to say thank you for reading my book. I hope I have inspired you to become a better YOU no matter how many twists and turns you have in life enjoy life's roller-coaster. This is the first part of my journey.

Book two is in the process of being written now, the next part of my autobiography tells you how I moved forward from the life I had to the life I want by taking ACTION.

Until next time......

Best Wishes
Maxine   x

ABOUT THE AUTHOR

$\mathbf{M}$axine English is a single mother of two teenagers from Essex, United Kingdom. Her Entrepreneurial journey started in March 2011 when her husband nearly beat her to death in front of her two children. That was the worst day of her life that turned into her best day. It changed her as a person, she became more ambitious and determined than ever before to make a great life for herself and her two children, taking herself further than ever before.

Being on heavy pain killers to conceal the pain of her bruises and two crushed vertebra that he left her with after a severe beating. She thought that day was going to be her last while her children watched in horror. Maxine decided that he may have broken her back, but he was not going to break her spirit. She lay there for months letting her body heal and her bruises fade. She wrote a detailed business plan to give herself a goal to work towards. There was a gap in the market and she was determined to fill it.

Within a few months she was back at work however, due to her spinal injury she only worked a few months before she was back on the sick. Maxine was told she was lucky not to be in a wheel chair with the injury she had sustained. But she'd come this far Maxine wasn't going to give up now

Determined not to live her life in the shadow of her former self in September 2014 she built up her physical and emotional strength and went back to college to study a Level 2 Diploma in Biology, Chemistry, Physics and Forensics. Getting a distinction star in all subjects, but she wanted to push herself further, so Maxine also studied level 2 in Maths and English at the same time within a year. She came top of her class in both subjects giving her the confidence boost she needed to move to the next level.

Maxine had already been told she was unemployable, so she

started her own business Party Crown Direct in 2015. Her physical shop opened in December 2015 in Essex, UK and has since moved the whole business online www.partycrowndirect.co.uk

By doing this Maxine now has the time for her other passion of helping others through their challenges in life and coaching them to overcome their adversities.

Maxine has been on TV including Channel 4, Channel 5, Living, More4 and E4. Been in Closer magazine and in the Sun to share her stories to help others about body confidence. Maxine has also been interviewed numerous times on Facebook and been on the Radio about what she has been through.

Maxine wears many hats from being a Business Owner, Entrepreneur, an author of "Broken, Abused Left for DEAD" an award winning motivational and transformational Public Speaker standing on many stages. She has been the head of broadcasting, interviewing other Business owners, Multi-millionaires and Celebrities on Inspired to Achieve Global TV.

A life and confidence coach, magazine contributor and she was also one of Bradley Chapman's Divisional Director "The 12" at Yes You Can Inspired to Achieve. She is making it her life's mission to put a stop to Domestic Violence, bullying and other negative influencers. She is doing it through standing on stage, broadcasting and coaching to help others overcome everything in their past/present and to help them move forward to a better future. Helping woman, children and men from all walks of life not to live in FEAR, have confidence and build their self-esteem.

Maxine English is The **FEAR FIGHTER.**

Printed in Great Britain
by Amazon